Paradoxes from A to Z

Paradoxes from A to Z, third edition is the essential guide to paradoxes, and takes the reader on a lively tour of puzzles that have taxed thinkers from Zeno to Galileo, and Lewis Carroll to Bertrand Russell. Michael Clark uncovers an array of conundrums, such as Achilles and the Tortoise, Theseus' Ship, and the Prisoner's Dilemma, taking in subjects as diverse as knowledge, science, art and politics. Clark discusses each paradox in non-technical terms, considering its significance and looking at likely solutions.

This third edition is revised throughout, and adds nine new paradoxes that have important bearings in areas such as law, logic, ethics and probability.

Paradoxes from A to Z, third edition is an ideal starting point for those interested not just in philosophical puzzles and conundrums, but anyone seeking to hone their thinking skills.

Michael Clark is Emeritus Professor of Philosophy at the University of Nottingham, UK. He is editor of the leading journal *Analysis*, and has published widely in a variety of areas, including philosophical logic and the philosophy of law.

Praise for the first edition:

'Self-contained courses in paradox are not usually taught as part of a philosophy degree. There is good reason for thinking they should be, and this book would make the ideal text for just such a course.'

Times Higher Education Supplement

'Clark's survey is an entertaining junkshop of mind-troubling problems.'

The Guardian

'*Paradoxes from A to Z* is a clear, well-written and philosophically reliable introduction to a range of paradoxes. It is the perfect reference book for anyone interested in this area of philosophy.'

Nigel Warburton, author of *Philosophy: The Basics*

'An excellent book . . . Clark's masterful discussion makes this one of the best general introductions to paradoxes.'

James Cargile, *University of Virginia*

'Very well done . . . a useful complement to the existing literature.'

Alan Weir, *Queen's University Belfast*

Paradoxes from
A to Z

Third edition

MICHAEL CLARK

Routledge
Taylor & Francis Group

LONDON AND NEW YORK

First published 2002
by Routledge

Second edition published 2C
Reprinted 2010 (twice)

Third edition published 201
by Routledge
2 Park Square, Milton Park,

Simultaneously published ir
by Routledge
711 Third Avenue, New York, NY 10017

Routledge is an imprint of the Taylor & Francis Group, an informa business

© 2012 Michael Clark

The right of Michael Clark to be identified as author of this work has been asserted by him in accordance with sections 77 and 78 of the Copyright, Designs and Patents Act 1988.

British Library Cataloguing in Publication Data
A catalogue record for this book is available from the British Library

Library of Congress Cataloging in Publication Data
Clark, Michael, 1940–
    Paradoxes from A to Z / by Michael Clark. – 3rd ed.
        p. cm.
    Includes bibliographical references and index.
    1. Paradox. 2. Paradoxes. I. Title.
    BC199.P2C57 2012
    165–dc23   2012010326

ISBN13: 978-0-415-53857-2 (pbk)
ISBN13: 978-0-203-09641-3 (ebk)

Typeset in Rotis by Keystroke, Codsall, Wolverhampton

MIX
Paper from responsible sources
FSC
www.fsc.org   FSC® C004839

Printed and bound in Great Britain by the MPG Books Group

Contents

Contents

Contents

Contents

Foreword to the Third Edition

Nine new entries have been added to those in the Second Edition. Four of them relate to the law: **Murder,** the **Poison Hypothetical,** the **Prosecutor's Fallacy,** and the **Red Taxi Paradox.** The others are the much discussed **Paradox of Future Generations, Pascal's Wager,** a new paradox involving infinite series, the **Pasadena Paradox,** the Newcomb-like **Dr Psycho Paradox** and the **Trolley Problem.** There are now 94 entries altogether.

Some minor corrections have been made and the reading lists updated and expanded. I should like to thank Peter Cave, Isabel Gois, Bob Kirk, and especially Nicholas Shackel for their comments.

Preface

Pick up a recent issue of a philosophical journal like *Mind* or *Analysis* and it is surprising how many of the papers you see there are about philosophical paradoxes. Philosophy thrives on them, and many have borne abundant fruit. As Quine says, 'More than once in history the discovery of paradox has been the occasion for major reconstruction at the foundation of thought'. The development of nineteenth-century mathematical analysis (Zeno's paradoxes), twentieth-century set theory (the paradoxes of set theory), the limitative theorems of Gödel, and Tarski's theory of truth (the liar group) are dramatic illustrations.

The term *paradox* is given a very broad interpretation in this book, far broader than will appeal to many logical purists. Any puzzle which has been called a 'paradox', even if on examination it turns out not to be genuinely paradoxical, has been regarded as eligible for inclusion, though the most fascinating are among those recognized by the purist, those which appear to be perennially controversial. For a brief discussion of the notion see the entry **Paradox**, p. 159.

This A to Z is a personal selection. But with the exception of two small groups, the well-known philosophical paradoxes will be found here, along with others less familiar or else recently propounded. The first missing group contains a few rather technical set-theoretic paradoxes like Burali–Forti and Zermelo–König, and those of Schrödinger and time-travel involving advanced physics. The other group includes paradoxes I regard as trivial, like the paradox of the omnipotent god who cannot make a stone so heavy that he can't lift it, and near duplicates of some already included. Most of those discussed concern motion, infinity, probability, sets, inference, identity, rationality, knowledge and belief, though there are some from the fields of ethics, political theory and aesthetics.

Preface

One entry at least is not a paradox at all, but helps to address the question of what a paradox is.

I have sought to avoid technicality, but many of the most fascinating paradoxes involve infinity, and here it is not possible to avoid technicality completely; the same applies to some of the entries on logical inference. I have tried to explain the basic ideas in simple terms, but if they are still not to your taste there are plenty of wholly non-technical entries to move on to. Most entries are self-contained, although there are frequent cross-references. Where one entry depends on another, this is indicated: for example, the entries on Cantor's and Richard's paradoxes presuppose that those on Galileo's paradox and Hilbert's hotel have been read first, and that on plurality presupposes Galileo's, Hilbert's and Cantor's.

For some paradoxes, for example the Zeno paradoxes of **Achilles and the Tortoise, The Arrow** and **The Racecourse,** there is now a broad consensus about their resolution. This is also true of the statistical illusions, like **Bertrand's Box, Monty Hall, The Xenophobic Paradox** and **Simpson's.** But often the most frivolous-seeming of puzzles turn out to have an unexpected depth and fecundity. It is a mark of such paradoxes (which include **The Liar** group and **The Heap**) that not only is their resolution persistently controversial but their significance is also a matter of debate. The suggested resolutions offered for them here should be read with their controversial nature in mind.

There are two cases in which I have had to provide my own name for a paradox: those I call 'The Paradox of Jurisdiction' and 'The Xenophobic Paradox'. A happy consequence was that they enabled me to include paradoxes for the letters 'J' and 'X', which might otherwise have lacked an entry.

Cross-references to other paradoxes are indicated in bold. Items marked with an asterisk in the *Further Reading* lists are of a more advanced, and often technical, nature.

Acknowledgements

Thanks to Hao Wang, Stephen Yablo and Zeno for giving their names to paradoxes, and providing entries for 'W', 'Y' and 'Z'.

I am grateful to Robert Black, Bob Kirk, Jeff Ketland and John Perry for suggestions and comments, and I have a special debt to Peter Cave, Paul Noordhof, Nick Shackel, Nigel Warburton and two anonymous readers.

If only to provide an example for the paradox of The Preface, I have to acknowledge my own responsibility for the errors this book will inevitably contain.

I am grateful to a former editor of *Cogito* for permission to reproduce material from my article 'An introduction to infinity', 1992. I have also reproduced material from the appendix to my paper 'Recalcitrant variants of the liar paradox', *Analysis*, 1999, vol. 59 (of which I retain the copyright). Ashley Langdon kindly gave permission to use his program to generate the graph on p. 164 from his website.

Achilles and the Tortoise

$$d_1 \qquad\qquad\qquad\qquad d_2 \qquad\qquad d_3 \quad d_4 \; d_5$$

Achilles runs faster than the tortoise and so he gives it a head start: Achilles starts at d_1 and the tortoise at d_2. By the time Achilles has made up the tortoise's head start and got to d_2, the tortoise is at d_3. By the time Achilles has got to d_3 the tortoise has reached d_4. Each time Achilles makes up the new gap the tortoise has gone further ahead. How can Achilles catch the tortoise, since he has infinitely many gaps to traverse?

This is perhaps the most famous of the paradoxes of Zeno of Elea (born *c.* 490 BC).

Summing an Infinite Series

Of course we know that Achilles will catch the tortoise. He completes the infinitely many intervals in a finite time because each successive interval, being smaller than the one before, is crossed more quickly than its predecessor. Suppose Achilles catches the tortoise after running a mile. The infinitely many smaller and smaller intervals he traverses have to add up to a mile. But how can that be?

It wasn't until the nineteenth century that a satisfactory mathematical way of summing the intervals was developed. The solution was to define the sum of an infinite series as the *limit* to which the sequence of its successive partial sums converges. For simplicity, suppose they both proceed at a uniform speed, and that Achilles goes only twice as fast as the tortoise, giving him a half-mile start. (The principle is the same if Achilles' speed is, more realistically, much greater than twice the tortoise's, but the assumption of a dilatory Achilles makes the arithmetic simpler.)

By the time Achilles has made up this head start, the tortoise has gone a further quarter-mile. When he has gone this further quarter-mile the tortoise is a furlong (one-eighth of a mile) ahead, and so on. Then the intervals Achilles traverses, expressed as fractions of a mile, are $\frac{1}{2}$, $\frac{1}{4}$, $\frac{1}{8}$, $\frac{1}{16}$, ... The partial sums are

$\frac{1}{2}$ mile

$\frac{1}{2} + \frac{1}{4} = \frac{3}{4}$ mile

$\frac{1}{2} + \frac{1}{4} + \frac{1}{8} = \frac{7}{8}$ mile

$\frac{1}{2} + \frac{1}{4} + \frac{1}{8} + \frac{1}{16} = \frac{15}{16}$ mile

and so on.

So the sequence of partial sums will go:

$\frac{1}{2}$, $\frac{3}{4}$, $\frac{7}{8}$, $\frac{15}{16}$, $\frac{31}{32}$, $\frac{63}{64}$, $\frac{127}{128}$, $\frac{255}{256}$, $\frac{511}{512}$, $\frac{1023}{1024}$, $\frac{2047}{2048}$, $\frac{4095}{4096}$, . . .

It goes on for ever, getting closer and closer ('converging') to 1. In this case 1 is the limit, and so the sum, of the series. Achilles gradually closes in on the tortoise until he reaches it.

More precisely, but in more technical terms, take any number ε greater than 0: then there will be some term in the sequence of finite sums, call it S_j, such that every term from S_j onwards is within ε of the limit. For example, suppose ε is $\frac{1}{8}$. Then every term of the sequence from $\frac{15}{16}$ onwards is within $\frac{1}{8}$ of the limit, 1. If ε is $\frac{1}{1000}$, every term from $\frac{1023}{1024}$ is within $\frac{1}{1000}$ of 1. And so on.

Thomson's Lamp

With Achilles and the tortoise the appearance of paradox arose from the seeming impossibility of completing an infinite series of tasks, a 'supertask'. The following example of a lamp, proposed by the late James Thomson, is a vivid illustration. The lamp is switched on and off alternately: the first switching takes place at $\frac{1}{2}$ minute, the second after $\frac{3}{4}$ minute, and so on. Every time it is switched on it is then switched off, and vice versa. The supertask is completed one minute after it is started. Of course this particular supertask can't physically be performed, but is it impossible in principle? At first Thomson thought he could generate a contradiction out of this description by asking whether the lamp was on or off at one minute: it couldn't be off, because whenever it was turned off it was immediately turned on again, nor could it be on, for a similar reason. But the description of the supertask entails nothing about the lamp's state at one minute, since each switching in the unending series occurs before one minute is up.

Perhaps it stretches our notion of *task* to breaking point to suppose that there is no lower limit whatsoever to the time a task can take. But then the use of the term 'task' for each of Achilles' traversals is tendentious. The claim is only that Achilles can be regarded as having traversed infinitely many intervals in catching the tortoise.

Why, then, is Achilles at the limit, 1, after his infinitely many traversals? After all, none of them gets him to 1, since there is no last traversal. The answer is that, if he is anywhere – as he surely is – he must be at 1, since he can neither be short of 1 nor beyond it. He cannot be short of 1 because he would then still have some – indeed, infinitely many – traversals to make, having so far only made finitely many of the traversals. And he cannot be beyond 1, since there is no interval from 1 to any point beyond 1 which is covered by the traversals.

See also The Arrow, The Paradox of the Gods, The Tristram Shandy, The Spaceship, The Racecourse.

Further Reading

Paul Benacerraf, 'Tasks, super-tasks, and the modern Eleatics', *Journal of Philosophy*, 1962, vol. 59, reprinted in Wesley C. Salmon, *Zeno's Paradoxes*, Indianapolis, Ind., Bobbs-Merrill, 1970. Salmon's anthology contains other illuminating papers.

A. Grünbaum, *Modern Science and Zeno's Paradoxes*, Middletown, Connecticut, Wesleyan University Press, 1967.

R. M. Sainsbury, *Paradoxes*, 3rd edn, Cambridge, Cambridge University Press, 2009, chapter 1.

Wesley C. Salmon, *Space, Time and Motion*, Enrico, California and Belmont, California, Dickenson Publishing Co., Inc., 1975, chapter 2.

Allais' Paradox

You are offered a choice between (1) getting £400 and (2) having a 50% chance of winning £1,000. Although the expected utility of the latter, namely £500, is greater than that of the former, you are more likely to choose (1). A 100% chance of £400 is more attractive than a 50% chance of £1,000 to generally reasonable people.

Up to a point, people who are generally reasonable and prudent prefer a certain gain to an uncertain one with greater expected utility (EU). Thus, (1) they prefer a certain £400 to a 0.5 chance of £1,000, the expected utility of which is £500.

(2) A case involving two choices shows again the psychological advantage of certainty:

A Chance of £2m = 1.0	EU = £2m

B 0.1 chance of £10m	EU = £2.78m
0.89 chance of £2m	
0.01 chance of £0	

In B, we get the EU by multiplying the probability by the value for each of the three chances and adding the results together. So we get EU = (0.1 × 10) + (0.89 × 2) + (0.01 × 0) million pounds. (See the **Two-Envelope Paradox** for further explanation.) Most people prefer A to B, because they prefer the certainty of £2m to an uncertain outcome with a greater EU.

C 0.11 chance of £2m	EU =	D 0.1 chance of £10m	EU =
0.89 chance of £0	0.22m	0.9 chance of £0	£1m

But most people prefer D to C (the 0.01 extra chance here of £0 in D has no significant effect) – which is not consistent with the first choice.

(3) Given the choice between a certain £2m (EU = £2m) versus a 0.98 chance of £10m and a 0.02 chance of £0 (EU = £9.8m), most people prefer the certainty of the first to the second, although the latter has much greater EU.

But they prefer 0.98 of £10m to 0.01 of £2m, because, in the absence of certainty and a very much higher EU for the former, their psychological values follow probability.

Again, up to a point, people will avoid great loss, however great the expected gain.

(4) A comfortably-off person will prefer a 0.999999999 chance of £2m and a 0.000000001 chance of ruin to a 0.999999999 chance of ruin and 0.000000001 chance of gain, *however great the gain*. (Cf. the Sure Loss Principle in the **St Petersburg Paradox**.)

Suppose, for example, the gain were so huge that a tiny chance of it still had a very high EU. For example, suppose the expected gain were a billion (10^9) pounds. This is a 0.000000001 (10^{-9}) chance of a quintillion pounds, a quintillion being a million trillion or 10^{18}. He will still prefer the virtual certainty of £2m. Allais asks rhetorically, 'Who could claim that such a man is irrational? He accepts the first because it gives him a practical certainty of gaining [£2m] and refuses the second because it gives him a practical certainty of being ruined' (Allais, 532, my translation. We ignore here any complication arising from the diminishing marginal utility of money.)

Reasonable, prudent people 'begin in effect by fixing a maximum loss which they do not want in any case to exceed, then they choose by comparing their expected mathematical gain with their chance of ruin, but here it is not a case of mathematical expected gain M of monetary values g, but of mathematical expectation μ of psychological values γ . . .' (533).

In short, people who are generally quite rational tend to be attracted to certainty and averse to loss in the face of mathematical utilities to the contrary, and it would be a mistake to follow the mathematics in our economic planning in ignorance of the psychology. Once this is recognized, the paradox dissolves, but it has helped to teach us an important lesson.

These cases are taken from Allais' paper (referenced below). Maurice Allais, a distinguished French economist and physicist born in 1911, became a Nobel Laureate in Economics in 1988.

A further type of example is given by Kahneman and Tversky, who offer the following 2-stage example:

Stage 1: 0.25 chance of moving to 2nd stage.
Stage 2: Choice between
   A. sure win of $30;
   B. 0.8 chance $45, 0.2 chance of nothing.

You must first choose for both stages. For the second stage, most people will choose A.

When presented in the equivalent, 1-stage, form:

A' 0.25 chance of $30, 0.75 chance of nothing;
B' 0.2 chance of $45, 0.8 chance of nothing;

most people will choose B'.

The authors explain this in terms of an 'isolation effect': in the first case people simplify by ignoring the first stage, since it is common to both options, and go for the certainty of $30.

Further Reading

*M. Allais, 'Le comportment de l'homme rationnel devant le risque', *Econometrica*, 1953, vol. 21. (Has English summary at the beginning.)

Daniel Kahneman, *Thinking, Fast and Slow*, London, Allen Lane, 2011.

*Daniel Kahneman and Amos Tversky, 'Prospect theory: an analysis of decision under risk,' *Econometrica*, 1979, vol. 47.

The Paradox of Analysis

We can analyse the notion of brother by saying that to be a brother is to be a male sibling. However, if this is correct, then it seems that it is the same statement as 'To be a brother is to be a brother'. Yet this would mean the analysis is trivial. But surely informative analysis is possible?

This paradox is associated with G. E. Moore (1873–1958), but the problem arose in the work of Gottlob Frege (1848–1925), and it can be traced back to the Middle Ages.

Consider

(1)   A brother is a male sibling
(2)   Lines have the same direction if and only if they are parallel to one another.

If these analyses are correct then 'brother' and 'male sibling' are synonymous, and so are the expressions for the analysed and analysing notions in the second example. Yet to say (1) is not the same as to say that a brother is a brother – any more than saying (2) is saying that lines have the same direction when they have the same direction.

The paradox poses a threat to the possibility of giving an analysis of a concept, the threat that such an analysis must be either trivial or wrong.

But are 'brother' and 'male sibling' precisely synonymous? As Moore points out, it would be correct to translate the French word *frère* as 'brother' but not as 'male sibling'. And it seems that someone could believe that Pat is a brother without believing he was a male sibling, or believe that two lines had the same direction without believing they were parallel to one another. What then makes an analysis correct? Can examples like (1) and (2) be correct

9

analyses unless the analysing expression is synonymous – at least in a coarse-grained way – with the expression for that which is being analysed? It seems not, at least if we are concerned with the analysis of concepts.

So what makes (1) and (2) more informative than their trivial counterparts, 'A brother is a brother', etc.? The answer is surely that different concepts are employed in analysing the concept in question: the notion of *brother* is explained in terms of the two different concepts, those of *sibling* and *male*; (more interestingly) the notion of *same direction* is explained in terms of the notion of *being parallel*. If you had the concept of brother but not the more general concept of sibling, you could believe that Pat was a brother without believing that he was a male sibling. If you lacked the concept of parallel lines you could believe two lines had the same direction without believing that they were parallel to one another.

Frege famously pointed out that the same object, the planet Venus, could be referred to by expressions with different senses, 'the Morning Star' and 'the Evening Star'. The senses are different 'modes of presentation' of the same planet. Analogously, the senses of 'brother' and 'male sibling' can be recognized as the same, but presented differently by the two expressions. So analysis can be informative by presenting the same sense in terms of different concepts.

It is only fair to add that there is widespread contemporary scepticism, inspired principally by the late W. V. Quine, about a notion of synonymy which would support conceptual analysis.

Further Reading

Thomas Baldwin, *G. E. Moore*, London and New York, Routledge, 1990, chapter 7.

G. E. Moore, 'A reply to my critics', in P. A. Schilpp, ed., *The Philosophy of G. E. Moore*, Chicago and Evanston, Ill., Northwestern University Press, 1942.

The Arrow

An arrow cannot move in the place in which it is not. Nor can it move in the place in which it is. But a flying arrow is always at the place at which it is. Therefore, it is always at rest.

This is another of Zeno's paradoxes.

If an arrow is moving, it cannot move in the place where it is, since it is only there at an instant. Since movement is change of place over time, the arrow moves during an interval of time: it cannot move during an instant of time, since an instant has no duration. Doesn't this mean that the arrow is at rest at every instant, and so never moves? If so, everything is likewise always at rest, and there is no such thing as motion.

Though the arrow cannot move *during* an instant of time, it does not follow that it cannot be moving *at* an instant. It's a matter of what it's been doing before and after that instant. If you are asked what you were doing at midday on Sunday it makes perfectly good sense to reply that you were mowing the lawn. If Zeno had been right, there could be no such activity as mowing the lawn, since that involves motion. You can't, of course, have done any mowing during that instant; rather, at that moment, you were in the course of mowing. Thus the flying arrow is in the course of moving at any instant included in a stretch of time during which it is moving. The arrow is moving at an instant, i, if it is in different positions at nearby instants before and after i (or, to put it more accurately, at arbitrarily close positions at arbitrarily close instants). And it is at rest at an instant only if there is an interval of time, containing that instant, during which it does not change its position.

Now if the arrow is moving at a given instant there must surely be some speed at which it is moving. Its average speed is the distance it travels divided by the time it takes. But its speed at an instant cannot be calculated in this way, since that would involve an illicit division by 0. So how can it have a speed at an instant? It needed the mathematical developments of the nineteenth century to make sense of how fast it is travelling at a given instant i. Speed at an instant i is identified with the limit of average speeds during intervals converging to 0 and containing i. The simplest case is when the arrow is flying at a constant speed during such intervals: then it will be travelling at that speed at each instant during those intervals. For the notions of limit and convergence see **Achilles and the Tortoise.**

See also **The Racecourse, The Spaceship, The Paradox of the Gods.**

Further Reading

Wesley C. Salmon, *Space, Time and Motion*, Enrico, California and Belmont, California, Dickenson Publishing Co., Inc., 1975, chapter 2.

The Barber Shop Paradox
(The Paradoxes of Material
Implication)

Allen, Brown and Carr work in a barber's shop. At least one of them has to stay in to mind the shop. So

(1) If Carr is out, then if Allen is out, Brown is in.

Allen is too nervous to go out without Brown. So

(2) If Allen is out, then Brown is out too.

It seems to follow that Carr can never go out. But this can't be right: Carr can be out provided Allen is in.

This comes from Lewis Carroll's (C. L. Dodgson's) *Symbolic Logic*. We can abbreviate the argument as follows:

(1) If C, then if A then not-B.
(2) If A then B.
So (3) not-C.

It seems that, if (2) is true, then the consequent, or main 'then' clause, of (1) is false: doesn't *if A then not-B* contradict *if A then B*? But then the antecedent, or principal 'if' clause, of (1), namely C, will be false too. (For, if it is true that *if p then q* but false that *q*, then it must be false that *p*.) Hence (3).

But surely the two premisses do not really require Carr to be in. Both premisses can be true when Carr is out and Allen is in. For, if Allen is in, there is at least one man in to mind the shop, and, whether Brown is in or out, Allen hasn't gone out without him. What has gone wrong with the argument of the last paragraph?

13

Although *if A then not-B* appears incompatible with *if A then B*, arguably it is not (though many logicians dispute this). Provided A is false, both can be true together. To see this, consider the following case. Dennis has applied for a job with a certain company but, with his experience and ambition, he will not work for it unless he is made a director. So *if he works for the company he will be a director*. But the company has enough directors and is unwilling to appoint any more. So *if he works for the company he won't be a director*. Clearly Dennis will not work for the company, for if they offer him a post it will be in a non-directorial position, and he won't accept that. It is because we know both of the italicized conditionals that we know that Dennis won't work for the company.

So the argument of the opening paragraph breaks down and C is not excluded by (1) and (2) but is compatible with them. Despite first appearances, it does not follow from (1) and (2) that Carr is never out.

An Analogous Geometrical Argument

Carroll reported that someone had sent him the following geometrical analogue of the paradox. In the figure angle *a* = angle *b*.

A: points *K* and *N* coincide
(so that the figure is a triangle).
B: angle *a* = angle *b*.
C: lines *KL* and *NM* are unequal.

(1) If C, then if A then not-B, becomes:

(1′) If lines *KL* and *NM* are unequal, then if *K* coincides with *N*, angles *a* and *b* are not equal.

(2) If A then B, becomes:

(2′) If K and N coincide, then angle a = angle b.

As Carroll notes, (1′) is proved in Euclid I.6. 'The second', he says, 'needs no proof'. After all, it is a given that the angles in the figure are equal, so they are equal whether or not the points coincide. The lines can be unequal when K and N don't coincide, whether or not the angles at the base are equal. In other words, (1′) and (2′) do not rule out the inequality of KL and NM: (3′), not-C, does not follow from (1′) and (2′).

Some might argue that a different sense of 'if' is involved in cases like this, though intuitively the senses seem the same. Then the onus is on them to show that they differ, for senses ought not to be multiplied without necessity.

Material Implication

In classical modern logic it is usual to formalize singular indicative conditionals like (2) above using *material implication*, though logicians are divided over whether this is wholly adequate or is merely the best available approximation in that logic. A statement, p, materially implies another, q, when it is not the case that both p and not-q. A common way of symbolizing material implication is by means of the horseshoe: $p \supset q$, read as 'p materially implies q'. A material implication is sometimes called a 'Philonian conditional', after the Stoic contemporary of Zeno, Philo of Megara, who had construed conditionals in this way.

There is a prima facie case for reading indicative conditionals as material implications. There does seem to be a way of deriving *if p then q* and *not-(p and not-q)* from one another. Consider

(2)   If Allen is out then Brown is out

(2m)   Allen is out $\supset$ Brown is out.

Using the definition of $p \supset q$ given above we can write (2m) as

It is not the case that Allen is out and Brown is not out.

Clearly this follows from (2), for (2) precludes Allen being out with Brown in.

The converse seems to hold as well. Suppose (2m) is true and that Allen is out. Then Brown must be out too (for it is not the case that Allen is out and Brown is not). So from (2m) it follows that *if* Allen is out, then Brown is out, which is (2).

On the other hand, before treating this demonstration of the equivalence of $p \supset q$ and *if p then q* as conclusive, notice that on the definition of material implication as given above $p \supset q$ will be true whenever p is false, for, if p is false, p and not-q is also false, and its negation true. But it doesn't seem right to allow that 'if 2=5 then the earth has a moon' is true merely in virtue of the falsity of its antecedent ('if' clause). Similarly, $p \supset q$ will be true whenever q is true, for, if q is true, p and not-q is false, and its negation true. But it doesn't seem right to allow that 'if 2=5 then the earth has a moon' is true merely in virtue of the truth of its consequent ('then' clause). (These are the so-called paradoxes of material implication, which arise if you treat singular indicative conditionals as material implications.)

Nevertheless, if we treat (1) and (2) above as material implications, as we know that (in effect) Carroll himself did, then there can be no denying that C is compatible with them.

(1) If C, then (if A then not-B)   (1m) $C \supset (A \supset \text{not-}B)$
(2) If A then B   (2m) $A \supset B$

For suppose Carr is out (C) and Allen is in:

(1m) is true, because its consequent is true: it is not the case that Allen is out and Brown is out (*not-not-B*), because it is not the case that Allen is out.

(2m) is true, because its antecedent is false.

So *C* is true and so are (1m) and (2m). (1m) and (2m) can both be true together because $A \supset B$ is compatible with $(A \supset not\text{-}B)$: when Allen is in, both have false antecedents.

However, this does not show that formalizing indicative if . . . then . . . statements in terms of $\supset$ is wholly adequate to their logic. Clearly some of the principles that hold for one hold for the other, and that is all we need to bring out the erroneous reasoning in the barber shop paradox. It does not follow that every principle that holds for one holds for the other. From

(*if p then q, if p then not-q*) is a compatible pair

and

$(p \supset q, p \supset not\text{-}q)$ is a compatible pair

it does not follow that *if p then q* can be identified with $p \supset q$ and *if p then not-q* identified with $p \supset not\text{-}q$. There are many different compatible pairs. Nevertheless, it is true that anyone who wants to construe the indicative conditional as a material implication needs both of the pairs above to be compatible. The argument above may therefore contribute to her case, but that is the most that can be said. (Naturally, if the case for identification could be made out independently, the erroneous step in the barber shop argument would be nailed without further ado.)

Further Reading

C. L. Dodgson, *Lewis Carroll's Symbolic Logic*, ed. W. W. Bartley III, New York, Clarkson Potter, 1977.

*Frank Jackson, *Conditionals*, Oxford, Basil Blackwell, 1987.

Stephen Read, *Relevant Logic*, Oxford, Blackwell, 1988, section 2.3.

Berry's Paradox

'The least integer not describable in fewer than twenty syllables' is itself a description of nineteen syllables. So the least integer not describable in fewer than twenty syllables is describable in fewer than twenty syllables, because the quoted expression is such a description and has only nineteen syllables.

This paradox was reported in 1906 by Bertrand Russell, who attributed it to G. H. Berry of the Bodleian Library. It belongs to the family of semantic paradoxes discovered about the turn of the nineteenth and twentieth century, which also includes the **Heterological** paradox and **Richard's**. We may assume that it is only the non-negative integers that are in question here.

We could avoid the contradiction by distinguishing between levels of description, in line with some treatments of semantic paradoxes like **The Liar** and of logical paradoxes like **Russell's**. At level 0, integers would never be specified in terms of descriptions of the form 'the least integer describable in such-and-such a way'; only at higher levels would such descriptions be admitted, and they would only refer to descriptions at the level one below. So the description 'the least integer describable in fewer than twenty syllables' would not be admitted at level 0. At level 1 this phrase would be interpreted as meaning 'the least integer not describable at level 0 in fewer than twenty syllables'. Since it would not be a level-0 description itself, it would not be self-refuting.

On the face of it this solution seems ad hoc. However, it may be possible to resolve the paradox without appeal to different levels of description. The non-negative integers, or natural numbers (0, 1, 2, . . .) can be defined in terms of 0 and the notion of successor, where the successor of a number is the number which is one greater than it – the successor of 23 is 24, for example:

    0 is a number
    1 is the successor of the number defined in the last line
    2 is the successor of the number defined in the last line
    3 is the successor of the number defined in the last line
    and so on ad infinitum.

'The successor of the number defined in the last line' is a description of only fourteen syllables. 24, for example, will be described in this way by the line following the definition of 23. In general, any natural number can be described in this way by using an expression of fewer than twenty syllables. So there will be no least number you can describe in no fewer than twenty syllables for Berry's description to pick out. There will therefore be no number both describable and not describable in fewer than twenty syllables.

But though this solution is not ad hoc, it may well appear a cheat. After all, these descriptions do not pick out the numbers on their own, independently of the context in which they occur. If we were to make that context explicit in the descriptions, most of them would exceed nineteen syllables. However, this may not make the proposed resolution any worse than the appeal to levels of description: short of making the level of description numerically explicit every time, the level of 'describable' in the Berry expressions will be context-dependent. And in any case what we mean by 'level 2' or 'level 23', for example, is only intelligible in the context of their explanation. If context dependence is unavoidable anyway, it is no obstacle to this proposal.

Further Reading

James D. French, 'The false assumption underlying Berry's paradox', *Journal of Symbolic Logic*, 1988, vol. 53, offers the resolution given above.

Bertrand's Box Paradox

You choose one of three boxes at random. One contains two gold coins (GG), another two silver coins (SS) and the third has one gold and one silver (GS). Each box is divided into two halves, which you can open separately, and each half contains a coin.

What is the chance that you select the one with two different coloured coins? One-third, obviously.

But suppose you select a box and the first side you open reveals a gold coin. Then either you have GG or GS, so that it seems your chance of GS is a half. Equally, if the first coin is silver, either you have SS or GS, and again your chance of GS seems to be a half. But the first coin you see must be either gold or silver. So your chance of GS must have been a half.

3 boxes: Gold | Gold   Silver | Silver   One of each

Of course the chance of choosing the box with different coloured coins is only ⅓. The problem is to see what is wrong with the argument above.

The fallacy, as Bertrand himself pointed out, is to assume that if the first of the coins in the chosen box is gold the chance that the other is gold is the same as the chance that the other is silver. It isn't, the silver is less likely. You are twice as likely to see a gold coin first if your box is GG than if it is GS; so seeing that one of your coins is gold tells you it is twice as likely you have GG as GS. Similarly, seeing that one of your coins is silver tells you it is twice as likely you have SS as GS.

Imagine repeating the choice 3,000 times, the coins being restored to the boxes, which are shuffled out of your sight between selections. Each time you pick a box you look at the first coin, and inevitably find it is either gold or silver. If you accept the fallacious argument for each selection, you would expect to pick GS about 1,500 times, but you would be mistaken. In fact about 2,000 of your selections will be same-colour selections, GG or SS. Only about 1,000 will be GS.

J. Bertrand was a mathematician who published his *Calculs des Probabilités* in 1889. See the next entry for a more significant paradox from the same author.

Bertrand's (Chord) Paradox

What is the chance that a random chord of a circle is longer than the side of an inscribed equilateral triangle?

(1) The chords from a vertex of the triangle to the circumference are longer if they lie within the angle at the vertex. Since that is true of one-third of the chords, the probability is one-third.

(2) The chords parallel to one side of such a triangle are longer if they intersect the inner half of the radius perpendicular to them, so that their midpoint falls within the triangle. So the probability is one-half.

(3) A chord is also longer if its midpoint falls within a circle inscribed within the triangle. The inner circle will have a radius one-half and therefore an area one-quarter that of the outer one. So the probability is one-quarter.

A chord is a straight line joining the ends of an arc.

According to Laplace's Principle of Indifference, if there is reason to believe that it is equally possible that each of a number of cases should be a favourable one, the probability of an event is

$$\frac{\text{the number of favourable cases}}{\text{the total number of cases}}$$

For example, the chance of randomly selecting an ace from a pack of cards is $4/52$.

Bertrand uses the three different answers to argue that his question is 'ill-posed', because he doesn't think it is possible to choose randomly from among an infinite number of cases. For there are infinitely many different chords of a circle. Apart from diameters, chords are uniquely identified by their midpoints, and a circle contains infinitely many points. (To put it technically, each point can be specified by an ordered pair of real Cartesian coordinates.) How would you divide the number of favourable cases by infinity? As it stands Bertrand's question is certainly ill-posed. But can it be replaced by a well-posed question? In fact, it turns out that it can be replaced by indefinitely many different questions. The trouble with the original question is that it fails to specify *how* the chord is to be randomly selected.

(1) The first solution can be shown to be equivalent to the probability that a randomly selected point on the circumference lies between any two given vertices (say *B* and *C*) of the triangle. If you select two vertices, then in theory one-third of the chosen points will lie between them. Each chosen point is the end-point of a chord which goes to the other vertex (*A*). Since the vertices determine three arcs of the circumference of equal length, the probability must be one-third. You could simulate this empirically by tossing broom straws at a straight line, thought of as a straightened-out circumference, dividing the number of those that intersect the middle third of the line by the total of those that intersect the line at any point. Generally the outcome will more or less converge to one-third.

(2) Throw broom straws at random at the circumference of a small circle, ignoring those that fail to intersect the circumference twice. In theory half the straws should form chords longer than the side of the triangle, and reported empirical tests confirm this. You can make do with a single inscribed triangle and radius if you

rotate the straw about the chord's midpoint until it is parallel to *AB*. Again the probability can be proved equivalent to that of Bertrand's second case.

(3) Inscribe the diagram for the third case on a dartboard and throw darts randomly at the board. Each point chosen determines the midpoint of a chord. You might think that of the throws where the dart sticks, the proportion where the dart strikes within the inner circle should approach one-quarter. But what if the dart hits the centre of the bull's eye? There are infinitely many, indeed uncountably many, diameters which have that mid-point. So no probability can be determined in this case, since the number of favourable cases and the number of total cases will both be uncountable, yet clearly the probability is not 1.

If we set aside cases like (3), there are indefinitely many other cases yielding a different probability. But this does not show there is really no probability at all. When the method of random selection is adequately specified, a determinate answer is available. So the proper response to Bertrand's original question is: what is the mechanism for selecting the chord randomly? And in general there is no one method to be preferred.

Poincaré thought that in the absence of further specification we should choose (2), so that the chance that a randomly chosen chord belongs to one of two sets of congruent chords is the same as the chance that it belongs to the other. The examination of this sort of case led to the development of what is known as integral geometry, which is used in stereology, the three-dimensional interpretation of flat images. Stereology has significant practical applications in mineralogy and medicine.

J. Bertrand published this paradox in 1889. The solution given here (except for case 3) is set out in Louis Marinoff, *"A resolution of Bertrand's paradox', *Philosophy of Science*, 1994, vol. 61, where full proofs are given. For criticism, see *Nicholas Shackel, 'Bertrand's paradox and the principle of indifference', *Philosophy of Science*, 2007, vol. 74.

The Paradox of Blackmail

There is nothing illegal about asking someone for money,
nor is it illegal to threaten to report someone's theft. But if, for
example, you threaten to expose someone's crime unless she
pays you money, you are guilty of blackmail.

This case has the superficial appearance of a paradox, but, although
some philosophical and legal writers have labelled it 'the paradox
of blackmail', it doesn't really merit the name. Even if blackmail
were nothing but the simple combination of a threat and a demand,
it wouldn't give rise to a genuine paradox. This is easy to see if you
consider some parallel cases. It is not in itself illegal to be drunk
nor is it illegal to drive a car, but it is illegal to be drunk while
driving. It is not illegal for two adults to have consensual sexual
intercourse nor is it illegal for them to be seen together in a crowded
public park, but it is illegal for them to be seen together having
sexual intercourse in a crowded public park.

However, blackmail is not merely any combination of a threat
and a demand: the threat and the demand must be related in a
particular way. Blackmail is a demand backed by a threat. The
threat is made in order to make sure that the demand is met. If
the threat is made for some other reason, then this is not a case of
blackmail, as the following example makes clear. Suppose Arthur
notices his friend Barbara shoplifting. He is short of money and so
approaches her and asks her for some cash. He then tells her he is
going to report her. Barbara thinks she is being blackmailed, and
that if she gives him the money he will keep quiet. But Arthur will
report her even if she pays up, and he tells her this (and means it).
In this example Arthur certainly isn't blackmailing Barbara, despite
the fact that he is making a threat and is asking for money.

Blackmail arises only when a demand is actually backed by a threat. As she knows he is going to carry out the threat whatever happens, Barbara is under no pressure to give him money. Once you recognize that blackmail is not simply a threat plus a demand, then the alleged paradox of blackmail dissolves.

But does it matter whether or not there is a paradox of blackmail? Yes, it does, because, if there were a genuine paradox, then there would be no satisfactory way of justifying a law against blackmail while avoiding the paradox.

If one or more of the component acts involved in blackmail were itself illegal or ought to be, then it might seem that this would provide grounds for making blackmail illegal. The alleged paradox would obviously be avoided in such circumstances. For example, a blackmailer who threatens violence commits the separate offence of threatening violence, which is a crime whether or not the threat is made within the context of blackmail. But, as this example makes obvious, if the wrong involved in the threats themselves were the only wrong involved, then there would be no reason for the law to treat them separately as blackmail. Yet in cases like this the element of blackmail exacerbates the offence, so that there is more to the wrong than the threat of violence.

Where criminals are blackmailed, you might try to identify a further component of the blackmail in virtue of which it should be a crime. For example, in English law it is an offence to accept, or agree to accept, money for not disclosing information that might be of material help in enabling a prosecution (except when the money is reasonable compensation for loss caused by the offence). However, the reason why the blackmailer implies that he will take money for his silence is that he threatens to report the crime unless the victim pays up. The implication arises only because the demand is backed up by a threat and does not simply accompany it. It is difficult to see how there could be such an implication if the paradox were genuine and blackmail were simply a combination of unrelated components. But set that complication aside. The proposal would still not cover blackmail adequately, since you are guilty of blackmail as soon as you make the blackmail threat. A victim who neither pays up nor offers to do so has still been blackmailed. And, if the criminality of the extra component were enough to make blackmail of criminals an offence, there would once again be no need of a separate crime of blackmail in these cases.

In short, until you recognize that the alleged paradox of blackmail is really no paradox, you are not going to be able to give satisfactory reasons for making blackmail illegal.

The so-called 'paradox' of blackmail has its origins in a series of articles written in the 1950s by the distinguished academic criminal lawyer, Glanville Williams, although he himself did not describe it as a paradox.

Further Reading

Michael Clark, 'There is no paradox of blackmail', *Analysis*, 1994, vol. 54.

Joel Feinberg, *Harmless Wrongdoing*, vol. 4 of *The Moral Limits of the Criminal Law*, Oxford, Oxford University Press, 1988, pp. 238–76.

James Lindgren, 'Unravelling the paradox of blackmail', *Columbia Law Review*, 1984, vol. 84.

Saul Smilansky, *Ten Moral Paradoxes*, Oxford, Blackwell, 2007, chapter 4.

The Bridge

Socrates arrives at a bridge guarded by a powerful lord, Plato, and begs to be allowed to cross. Plato replies:

> I swear that if the next utterance you make is true I shall let you cross, but if it is false I shall throw you in the water.

Socrates replies:

> You are going to throw me in the water.

If Plato does not throw him in the water, Socrates has spoken falsely and should be thrown in; but if he is thrown in, Socrates has spoken truly and should not be thrown in.

This is Buridan's seventeenth sophism. (See Further Reading below.)

You would expect that the only difficulty that Plato might have in fulfilling his oath would be in knowing whether Socrates' utterance was true or not. But Socrates subtly manages to frustrate him.

Many philosophers, following Aristotle, have denied that future contingent propositions have a truth value. If this view were right, Socrates' utterance would not be true, since it is an utterance about something that may or may not happen in the future. But it would not be false either. However, Aristotle's view confuses truth with knowledge or predetermination. To say that it is true that Socrates will be thrown in the water is not to say that anyone yet knows whether he will or that it is already determined whether he will. Its truth or falsity depends on what Plato is going to do.

It is logically impossible for Plato to fulfil his oath in the circumstances. 'He has no obligation to keep it at all, simply because he cannot do so', Buridan concludes, reasonably enough.

Buridan's sophism is the most superficial of paradoxes, if it is to count as one at all. For it is merely an unusual case in which an oath cannot be fulfilled for reasons of logic.

(If Plato is free of any obligation, presumably he is free to throw Socrates in the water if he wishes. Interestingly, if we assume Plato is honourable, there is a way that Socrates can guarantee he doesn't get wet. He can say:

(U) Either I'm speaking falsely and you will throw me in, or I'm speaking truly and you won't throw me in.

If (U) is true, the first alternative is ruled out and the second alternative must be true: so Socrates is not thrown in.

If (U) is false, both alternatives must be false. And if the first alternative is false, since Socrates is speaking falsely it will be false that he will be thrown in.

Either way Socrates escapes a dousing.)

A variant of Buridan's sophism appears in Cervantes' *Don Quixote*. The Bridge has been traced back to Chrysippus (c. 280–c. 207 BC).

Further Reading

Jean Buridan, *Sophismata*, fourteenth century (undated), translation in *John Buridan on Self-Reference*, ed. and trans. G. E. Hughes, Cambridge, Cambridge University Press, 1982.

Compare the Pinnochio example in P. and V. Eldridge-Smith, *Analysis*, 2010, vol. 70 and P. Eldridge-Smith, *Analysis*, 2011, vol. 71.

Buridan's Ass

A hungry, thirsty donkey is sitting exactly between two piles of hay with a bucket of water next to each pile, but he has no reason to go to one side rather than the other. So he sits there and dies. But imagine that one of us were in a similar position between two tables of food and drink. Wouldn't we go to one of the tables rather than sit there and die?

If someone found himself midway between the food-laden tables, he would have no reason to go to one or the other. He might, it is true, consider tossing a coin. The trouble is that there would be nothing to make him associate heads with one table rather than another. Similarly, if he decided to choose on the basis of which of two birds reached a tree first: he would have no reason to associate a bird with a particular table.

This paradox is usually taken as a challenge to rationality. But Spinoza (1632–77), who was the first to associate it with Buridan, construed it as a challenge to causal determinism. Suppose that there is nothing in the animal's causal history to incline him to one table rather than the other. In that case, if all his actions are causally predetermined – the inevitable effects of prior causes, which themselves are produced by prior causes in a chain that goes back indefinitely – he will sit there and perish. If causal determinism is true of animals, we might expect it to apply to people as well. If everything that happens is determined by prior causes, a person would stay there and die. And it does seem possible in principle that he should find himself in such a position. If he did, wouldn't he always find some way of choosing a table to go to first rather than let himself starve to death? 'If I concede that he will [starve to death]', said Spinoza, 'I would seem to conceive an ass, or a statue of a man, not a man. But if I deny that he will, then he will determine himself, and consequently have the faculty of going where he wills and doing what he wills.'

Now causal determinism may not be true, but it is surely not overturned as easily as this.

Consider what we would say if we came across what, as far as we could tell, was a situation of this sort. If the man did go to one of the tables, we could not be sure that there was nothing un-detected in his causal history that explained his choice. If he stayed there and died, we would think he was suicidal or had gone mad. But then people do commit suicide, and they do go mad. In other words, in the unlikely event that you found yourself between the two tables with nothing to incline you to choose either table, you would either want to kill yourself or be in a situation where you were incapable of acting reasonably; and the latter seems very like madness. This, at any rate, was Spinoza's response: 'I grant entirely that a man placed in such an equilibrium . . . will perish of hunger and thirst. If they ask me whether such a man should not be thought an ass, I say that I do not know – just as I do not know how highly we should esteem one who hangs himself, or . . . fools and madmen . . .' (p. 490). So it looks as if the case of Buridan's ass fails to demolish causal determinism at a stroke.

Spinoza seems to have been wrong in attributing the example to Jean Buridan, the fourteenth-century philosopher and scientist who wrote extensively about many Liar-like paradoxes.

Further Reading

B. Spinoza, Appendix to *Ethics* 2, in *The Collected Works of Spinoza*, ed. and trans. Edwin Curley, Princeton, NJ, Princeton University Press, 1985.

The Cable Guy Paradox

The Cable Guy will come between 8 a.m. and 4 p.m. You choose whether to bet that he comes in the morning or the afternoon, and if he arrives in your interval I pay you $10, and otherwise you pay me $10. Before 8 a.m. there is no reason to prefer afternoon to morning. But there will be a time before his arrival when you will assign a higher probability to the afternoon. If he arrives in the morning, then however soon after 8 he arrives there will be a time after 8 but before his arrival when it will be rational to prefer the afternoon. Why wait till then? Why not bet on an afternoon arrival now?

More precisely, we divide the period from 8 to 4 into two four-hour intervals: (8, 12] and (12, 4), with both intervals open on the left. (If the first were not open on the left, the paradox would not arise, because the man could arrive at the stroke of 8.) In consequence, if the Cable Guy arrives precisely at noon the morning interval wins. In the absence of further information, it looks as if his arrival in either interval is equally likely. (The fact that the morning interval is closed on the right does not make it any longer.)

Suppose you bet on the morning interval. Whenever the man arrives, some part of the morning interval must have passed. Whenever he arrives there will be an earlier time at which the afternoon bet is preferable, since the afternoon interval will be longer than what remains of the morning interval after that time. On the other hand if you bet on the afternoon interval there will be no time before the arrival at which you should rationally prefer the morning bet.

Hájek puts the reasoning in terms of a principle he calls 'Avoid Certain Frustration', according to which you should not choose an option if you are sure that in future, if you are rational, you will prefer that you had made the other choice. Alternatively, betting on the morning interval, he says, is 'self-undermining' (116).

There is some idealization here, since if the Cable Guy comes a few nanoseconds after 8 there will not in practice be time before that for you to have the thought that you prefer the afternoon bet. But you can in advance argue that even in that case the afternoon bet would be preferable at some time before the arrival, and that can be known in advance.

Hájek notes that if you act on the principle and bet on the afternoon interval, any financial incentive, however small, to back the morning interval should change your choice – though there is no smallest such incentive. He also points out that there is no particular time you can be certain you will be frustrated. It is unclear whether these considerations make it easier to abandon the principles which generate the paradox, namely Avoid Certain Frustration and its equivalent in terms of self-undermining choices. Yet clearly we must abandon those principles if we are to avoid the paradox.

Further Reading

Alan Hájek, 'The Cable Guy paradox', *Analysis*, 2005, vol. 65, from which this entry is almost exclusively drawn.

Cantor's Paradox

The set of all sets, S, ought surely to be the biggest set of sets there is. But the power set of the set of all sets is bigger than S.

Common sense suggests that when there are infinitely many items of some sort, that is as many as there could possibly be. But there is a simple and very beautiful argument, due to Georg Cantor (1845–1918), to show that this is not the case, that there are, after all, bigger and bigger infinities. After much initial resistance, the argument came to be accepted by most working mathematicians but remains controversial to this day.

Now read **Galileo's Paradox** to see how to count infinite sets.

For any finite set you can get a bigger one by adding in a new member. For example, the set of the first 101 positive integers is bigger than the set of the first 100 positive integers. But this does not work with infinite sets. You cannot get a larger than denumerable set by adjoining a new member. (See the discussion of **Hilbert's Hotel**, which turns on the set of positive integers greater than 1 being the same size as the set of all the positive integers.) Similarly, the set of natural numbers, which has 0 and the positive integers as its members, is no bigger than the set of positive integers. In Galileo's paradox we saw that the set of squares of positive integers was denumerable, and so no smaller than the set of positive integers. Even if you adjoin denumerably many new members to a denumerable set, the result (called the *union* of the two sets) is still denumerable. Similarly it not difficult to show that the union of the set of positive integers and the set of negative integers is denumerable. Less obviously, the set of positive rational numbers (all the fractions) also turns out to be denumerable. Clearly there are denumerably many such fractions with a given denominator.

Imagine them listed in rows of increasing fractions, those with denominator 1 in the first row, those with denominator 2 in the second, and so on:

Then imagine tracing through them, starting with $1/1$, $2/1$, $2/2$, $1/2$, (back to top row) $3/1$, $3/2$, $3/3$, $2/3$, $1/3$, (back to top row) $4/1$, $4/2$, $4/3$, $4/4$, $3/4$, $2/4$, $1/4$,. . . . This gives us a linear enumeration: a first, a second, a third, and so on ad infinitum (skipping duplicates like $2/2$, which = $1/1$.) The rationals are paired off exhaustively with the positive integers in their normal ascending order. It begins to look as if common sense was right to stop at denumerable infinities. But Cantor showed otherwise.

Subsets and Power Sets

Crucial to Cantor's argument, in the simple form in which he eventually presented it, is the notion of the *power set* of a set, which is simply the set of its subsets. So, first, we need to explain the notion of subset. The set of Cabinet ministers, for example, is a subset of the set of Government ministers. In general, we say that x is a *subset* of y if and only if there is no member of x which is not a member of y. The definition is framed in this slightly awkward way to cover the case of the empty set, which is a subset of any set, y, since, having no members, it has no members which are not members of y. There is only one empty, or null, set, although it can be specified in many different ways, e.g. as the set of unicorns or the set of round squares. Sets can be distinct only if they differ in their membership. So there could not be two distinct empty sets, because they would both have the same members – none. Notice that a set counts as a subset of itself. It proves convenient to include this limiting case, and if we want to talk of a subset of y which is distinct from y we speak of a *proper* subset.

The power set of a set is the set of all its subsets. Consider the little set whose members are Tom and Dick. These two friends often dine at a certain restaurant on Friday evenings, and the head waiter always keeps a table for two ready for them each week. He knows that, although they often dine together, sometimes only one of them turns up, and occasionally neither appears. He is prepared for any of the four subsets: {Tom, Dick}, {Tom}, {Dick}, $\varnothing$. (The last symbol denotes the empty set.) To take another, only slightly larger, example, suppose that a lift operating in a three-storey building has three buttons inside, marked 'G', '1' and '2', for each of the floors. The designer of the electrical circuit connecting the buttons with the lift mechanism must consider all of the possible combinations of button presses if the lift is to function properly. He has to accommodate each of the subsets of the set of buttons {G, 1, 2}. It is not difficult to see that there are eight of these:

$$\{G, 1, 2\}, \{G, 1\}, \{G, 2\}, \{1, 2\}, \{G\}, \{1\}, \{2\}, \varnothing.$$

That is, all three buttons might be pressed at a particular stage, or any two, or any one, or none at all.

Every time you change a finite set by adding a member you double the number of subsets; because, in addition to all the original subsets, you have the sets formed by adding the new member to each of those original subsets. Indeed it is not difficult to prove that if a set has n members, where n is a finite integer, its power set has 2^n members. And, since 2^n is always greater than n, a finite set will always be smaller than its power set. Of course, there is an easier way of getting a bigger finite set than taking its power set: you just add in a new member. But this, as we have seen, will not work with infinite sets. (Compare **Hilbert's Hotel**.)

Bigger and Bigger Infinities

What Cantor was able to show was that the power set of x is always larger than x even when x is infinite. This is known as Cantor's theorem. His initial proof was rather involved, but in time he was able to produce a very simple, short and beautiful proof. To make it as accessible as possible I shall present a concrete example, and generalize from it.

Suppose that we have a set of people. Nothing will be said of its size: it may be finite, it may be infinite, and if infinite it may be countable (no larger than the set of positive integers) or uncountable. Its power set will contain all its subsets: think of all the collections of people that can be formed from the original set. (Note that each member of the original set will belong to many of the subsets in the power set.)

We show first that the set of people is smaller than or equal in size to its power set by showing how to pair off each person with a distinct collection (set) of people belonging to the power set. Recall that a set may have only one member (such sets are called *unit sets* or *singletons*): the one-membered sets {Tom} and {Dick}, for example, are two of the subsets of the set {Tom, Dick}. Now the power set of our set of people will include all the one-membered sets, to each of which will belong a single person. Match up each person with the unit set containing that same person and you have a one-to-one correlation between the set of people and a subset of its power set. So the power set is at least as large as the set of people. If we can show that the set of people is not the same size as its power set, it will follow that the latter is larger.

So we proceed to show that the set of people is not the same size as its power set. We do this by showing that there is no way of exhaustively pairing off respective members of these two sets one-to-one. For if they *were* the same size, there would be some way of pairing them, some order in which the respective members could be matched without residue. To show that there is none, we suppose that there is and then show that this supposition leads to a contradiction.

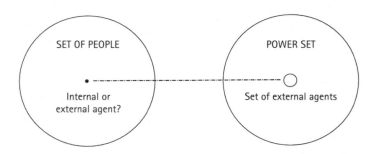

Suppose then that there is a one-to-one pairing of the requisite sort. To make the exposition more concrete, suppose that it takes the following form. Each collection (including the singletons and the empty set) of people in the power set is to have a unique agent selected from the original set, and every person in the original set is to be the agent of just one of the sets of people. Some collections, perhaps, can find enough money to pay someone outside their own group to act as their agent: they appoint an *external* agent. But some groups, perhaps, are too impecunious or mean to do this, and select one of their own number to act as agent: they appoint an *internal* agent. Of course, the empty set has no members to pay an agent, and so it has an unpaid volunteer, who must of course be external. Being the agent for the empty set of people is something of a sinecure, anyway, so that the lack of payment is no great sacrifice. (In any case, these details about payment merely add colour and are not needed for the argument.) There is bound to be at least one external agent, the agent for the empty set. And, if the original set of people has any members at all, then there will also be at least one internal agent, the agent for the subset which is the set of all the people. (Remember that a set is its own subset.)

The set of the external agents is of course a subset of the original set of people, and therefore belongs to its power set: so if the pairing we envisage is possible this set too will have an agent. She cannot belong to the set of people she represents, because only external agents belong to this set. But since she doesn't belong to the set, she is external and so does belong to it. We have a contradiction.

There is only one way out of this contradiction, and that is to recognize that it is impossible for such an agent to exist. But her existence followed from supposing that an exhaustive pairing was possible. Therefore that pairing must be impossible too.

The precise nature of the agent relation is not essential to this argument. All that matters is that we should consider a pairing which associates each person with a distinct set in the power set. A person is 'internal' if she is paired with a set containing that person; otherwise she is 'external'. The contradiction is elicited by considering the set of 'external' people.

Nor is it even essential to the argument that the members of the original set be people; they could be anything you like, provided we need make no assumption about the number in the set. Replace *person* by *element* in the paragraph above, and the argument still goes through. No exhaustive pairing of any sort is possible.

Finally, notice that the derivation of the contradiction does not depend on supposing that the members of the original set are matched with the members of the power set in any particular order. This is important, since if they could be exhaustively paired in some order or other, the sets would be equinumerous, so that we need to show that there is no such pairing for *any* ordering.

The power set of a set x, then, is always greater in cardinality than x, even when x is infinite. For, if the power set is at least as large as x and yet not equinumerous with it, it must be larger.

The Paradox

Now, finally, to the paradox. Cantor had shown that you can always get a bigger set by taking the power set of what you start with. Consider, then, the set of all the sets there are, which should be the biggest set whose members are all sets. By Cantor's theorem, its power set contains even more sets. The set of all sets is both the biggest and not the biggest set there is.

The moral is that the set of all sets is an illegitimate set. (But see Further Reading below.) For discussion see **Russell's Paradox**, which exposes another illegitimate set; indeed the argument for Russell's paradox was inspired by Cantor's proof.

Scepticism about Completed Infinities

At first sight this may all seem quite mind-boggling. So it is perhaps not all that surprising that established mathematicians of the day, including Cantor's own teacher Leopold Kronecker (1823–91), rejected his results, and this may well have contributed to his periods of depression. Later on, younger mathematicians came to his accept his work: for David Hilbert (1862–1943) it was 'the most admirable flowering of the mathematical spirit'. However, his results remain controversial, and have been rejected by the mathematical intuitionists led by L. E. J. Brouwer (1881–1966) and A. Heyting (1898–1980), whose followers continue to repudiate the conception of completed infinite wholes and cling to the Aristotelian idea of the infinite as the open-ended. On their view the paradox will not arise in the first place, of course.

Further Reading

A. W. Moore, *The Infinite*, 2nd edn, London and New York, Routledge, 2001, chapter 8.

*Paul Halmos, *Naïve Set Theory*, Princeton, NJ, Princeton University Press, 1960.

*Thomas Forster, *Set Theory with a Universal Set*, revised edn, Oxford, Clarendon Press, 1995, for set theories which admit the set of all sets by restricting the axiom of subsets.

The Paradox of the Charitable Trust

> Suppose you invest some money in a charitable trust. When the trust is terminated the income will go to an organization fighting famine and poverty. The money is expected to grow at a somewhat faster rate than famine and poverty.
>
> Suppose, too, that our present world will continue forever. Whatever date you choose for the trust to mature, there would be more money to help more people if you chose a later date. But if you let the trust grow forever, it will never be terminated to help anyone.

Maximizing utility in this case is impossible, since there is no maximum – until it is terminated, the trust continues to increase in value. The notion of satisficing, imported from economics, contrasts with that of maximizing expected utility. Satisficing involves choosing an alternative which, though it may not maximize expected utility, is good enough. One way of implementing this is to choose the first alternative you come across that you judge satisfactory.

In order to maximize expected utility you need to compute that utility and compare it with that of alternative options. These problems are avoided artificially in the example of the charitable trust because, for the sake of simplicity, we are assuming that more money relieves more human misery. But in many cases such a computation is impossible to perform, particularly as different sorts of utility are incommensurable: how do you compare the utility of reading a good short story with the pleasure of a backrub, for example? By satisficing in the manner described, you avoid these problems about computation and incommensurability. So it is not only in the unusual case of the charitable trust that satisficing has its merits. It is arguably not just an ad hoc solution to the present paradox.

There is one option that is clearly good enough and stands out as the right option. The value of the trust will increase at a compound rate faster than the famine and poverty, so that eventually the value of the trust will be sufficient to wipe them out. This will probably not be the first option that is good enough, so we had better not take the first as a matter of course. If the trust is not dissolved at the point of equal value it will go on to increase in value so that in addition to wiping out poverty etc. it can do further good. But, given that the aim of the trust was to fight poverty and famine, termination at this time is surely defensible. Once the fight has been won they can manage on their own.

The charitable trust example cries out for satisficing, whatever the general merits of that approach outside this context. How else can we avoid not terminating the trust and doing no good at all? But it is not ordinary satisficing, at least as it is described in the first paragraph above, since there is likely to be a much earlier time when terminating the trust will be good enough. But it must still count as satisficing of a sort, since maximizing is not possible here.

Because of the simplifying assumptions the example itself is somewhat unreal. But there will be examples in the real world which raise a similar problem.

Cliff Landesman was the first to draw attention to this paradox.

Further Reading

Michael Byron, 'Simon's revenge: or, incommensurability and satisficing', *Analysis*, 2005, vol. 65.

Cliff Landesman, 'When to terminate a charitable trust?', *Analysis*, 1995, vol. 55.

Dan Moller, 'Should we let people starve – for now?', *Analysis*, 2006, vol. 66.

The Chicken and the Egg

Which came first? Every chicken hatches from a chicken egg. But every chicken egg is laid by a chicken. So neither can come first. But surely one must.

Aristotle believed that species had always been around, and so had no beginning. So on his view neither would come first.

Now that we know that this is false, we have to solve the riddle empirically, by appeal to biology. Admittedly the notion of species has come in for criticism in recent years, and there are even those who deny their existence. But we set aside such scepticism.

One answer which has gained scientific popularity puts the egg first – 'no egg, no chicken':

A particular organism cannot change its own species during its lifetime. The change came about from a mutation when two organisms bred, producing a chicken egg. The egg preceded the chicken which hatched from it. So the egg came first.

On this view it doesn't matter who the parents were. Their species is not carried on through the egg because a mutation has taken place, and its genetic material determines the nature of the offspring. If it is a chicken egg, a chicken will hatch.

A competing answer puts it the other way round – 'no chicken, no egg':

Although the zygote results from both father and mother, the surrounding egg comes from the mother alone. Only a chicken can lay a chicken egg: so the chicken came first. (Waller in *Mind*, 1998.)

Waller says: 'To call any egg a chicken egg on account of its embryonic passenger is like calling the mother's uterus a chicken uterus on account of its delivering a chicken' (p. 852). He also points out that, unlike chickens, roosters are optional for egg producers.

On this view, presumably, a mutation takes place and produces a chicken (the zygote) as embryonic passenger, though it is inside an egg which is not a chicken egg. When it has hatched it will lay chicken eggs; but the chicken came first.

The puzzle is first mentioned by Plutarch (c. 46–c. 120).

Further reading

Aristotle, *Generation of Animals and History of Animals*.
Roy Sorensen, *A Brief History of the Paradox*, Oxford, Oxford University Press, 2003, p. 11. (A fascinating history.)
R. Teichmann, 'The chicken and the egg', *Mind*, 1991, vol. 100.
David Waller, 'The chicken and her egg', *Mind*, 1998, vol. 107.

Curry's Paradox

Using the self-referential statement (S) 'If it is true that S, then Paris is the capital of Italy', it seems that you can demonstrate the conclusion that Paris is the capital of Italy, or indeed anything you like. And the conclusion isn't even conditional on the truth of (S).

Assume the truth of (S), namely

(1)   It is true that S.

From (1), it follows that

(2)   S

From (2), by the definition of (S) we get

(3)   If is true that S, then Paris is the capital of Italy.

It follows from (1) and (3) by modus ponens (affirming the antecedent) that

(4)   Paris is the capital of Italy.

Since (4) follows from the assumption (1), we can incorporate the assumption in an 'if' clause, and assert on the basis of no assumption

(5)   If it is true that S, then Paris is the capital of Italy.

From (5) by the definition of (S)

(6)   S

From (6) it follows that

(7)   It is true that S

From (5) and (7) by modus ponens

(8)   Paris is the capital of Italy.

A parallel argument, substituting 'S_2' for 'S' to yield (S_2), 'If it is true that S_2, then Paris is not the capital of Italy', lets you prove that Paris is not the capital of Italy, and, if we combine the results of the two arguments, we have a contradiction on the basis of no assumptions.

Indeed, any statement, true or false, may be substituted uniformly in the argument above for 'Paris is the capital of Italy'. We can even substitute a contradiction and derive the contradiction in one go.

Paradox is avoided if 'provable' is substituted for 'is true', since the move from (6) to (7) then fails.

There is also a set-theoretic version of the paradox, which uses the unqualified comprehension principle (for which see **Russell's Paradox**).

For discussion see **The Liar**. One thing to notice in that discussion about this unusual variant of the liar is that it does not seem amenable to cogent resolution by appeal to dialetheism – not that dialetheism has a very extensive following yet, anyway. (See **The Liar** for an explanation of dialetheism.)

Further Reading

J.C. Beall, 'Curry's Paradox', *The Stanford Encyclopedia of Philosophy* (Fall 2008 edition), ed. Edward N. Zalta, http://plato.stanford.edu/archives/fall2008/entries/curry-paradox/.

*G. Boolos and R. Jeffrey, *Computability and Logic*, 4th edn, Cambridge, Cambridge University Press, 2002, pp. 236–38.

The Paradox of Democracy

Consider a democrat who favours monetary union. Suppose the majority in a referendum vote against monetary union. Then it appears that she is both for monetary union and, as a democrat, against it.

What distinguishes a democrat who favours monetary union from someone who favours it but is not a democrat? They may both vote in a democratic poll for it, since both want it enacted. What is distinctive of the democrat is that her order of preference is

(1) Democratically enacted monetary union
(2) Democratically enacted monetary separation
(3) Monetary union enacted undemocratically
(4) Monetary separation enacted undemocratically.

She prefers 1 to 2, and both of these to 3 and 4. Her democratic credentials are shown by her preference for 1 and 2 over 3 and 4, and her support for monetary union by her preference for 1 over 2 and 3 over 4. There is no inconsistency here.

Moreover, it is clear that she is not committed to the obviously untenable view that the majority is always right. Otherwise she could not consistently prefer 1 to 2 or 3 to 4. (Nor need she be committed to allowing the majority to oppress a minority, since in such cases she may prefer not to accept the democratic decision. Restricting democracy to protect minorities does not mean that the paradox cannot be propounded.)

But what if she is torn between her support for democracy and her support for monetary union? What if she is torn between 2 and 3? The situation is then like the situation in other normative conflicts. I promise to take my young daughter to a party but her brother falls over and splits his head open. I take my son to hospital and have to break my promise to my daughter. But I still have to make it up to her. The promise is not qualified by her brother's accident, it still stands. Or, to take a case where I am torn between the two, I promise to take my daughter to a party and my son to a film. The party was to be today, the film tomorrow, but both events are then postponed until 3 o'clock the day after tomorrow, so that I cannot keep both promises. I have conflicting obligations, both genuine. Even if it is irrational to have two conflicting factual beliefs (and the paradox of **The Preface** shows it may not always be), there is nothing irrational about two obligations which clash nor about having two political preferences which come into conflict.

Despite its name, the paradox is not particularly about democracy, but arises for the adherent of any other political system, e.g. monarchy or oligarchy. The analogue for a monarchist would give the following order of preference:

(1') Monetary union ordered by the monarch

(2') Monetary separation ordered by the monarch

(3') Monetary union contrary to the monarch's will

(4') Monetary separation contrary to the monarch's will.

The paradox was identified by Richard Wollheim ('A paradox in the theory of democracy', *Philosophy, Politics and Society* 2, ed. Peter Laslett and W. G. Runciman, Oxford, 1962). It differs from the paradox of the same name mentioned by Karl Popper: the possibility that the majority may vote for a tyrant to rule them, which is an interpretation of Plato's criticism of democracy suggested by Leonard Nelson.

Further Reading

Ross Harrison, *Democracy*, London, Routledge, 1993. He makes the point about conflicting normative beliefs.

Ted Honderich, 'A difficulty with democracy', *Philosophy and Public Affairs*, 1974, vol. 3, which inspired the treatment above.

Karl Popper, *The Open Society and its Enemies*, vol. I, London, Routledge & Kegan Paul, 1945, chapter 7, note 4.

The Designated Student

One of five students, called by the names of the weekdays, is to have a test. The one designated has a gold star pinned on her back while the others have silver stars. The teacher tells them the one chosen will not know in advance that she has been selected for the test. Monday to Friday are lined up in order one behind the other, with Friday at the back. Each student can see the backs of just those further up the line: Friday can see the backs of all the others, Thursday can see the backs of Wednesday, Tuesday and Monday, and so on. Everyone knows it can't be Friday, since Friday would see that none of those in front have the gold star. But then they know it can't be Thursday either, since Thursday knows Friday is out and none of the others had the gold star on their backs. And so on for Wednesday, Tuesday and Monday.

Yet obviously the teacher can give the surprise test.

Compare **The Unexpected Examination.** This paradox, due to Roy Sorensen, emphasizes that memory is irrelevant in this type of paradox. There is an argument similar to that for the second case discussed in the entry on **The Unexpected Examination** that any of Monday–Thursday can get the test without expecting it.

Further Reading

Roy Sorensen, *Blindspots*, Oxford, Clarendon Press, 1988, pp. 317–20.

The Paradox of Deterrence

If you can only deter an enemy by sincerely threatening retaliation which you know you will not want to carry out, since it will then be pointless and self-destructive, you will not be able to form the intention to retaliate because you know you won't fulfil it.

Suppose that the only likely way of warding off an enemy's aggression is to threaten devastating nuclear retaliation which would kill many innocent people and rebound back on you. In short, we are supposing that if the threat is ineffective you will have much to lose and nothing to gain by carrying it out. Then there is a problem for those who think this can be justified, if it is clear that attempting to bluff the enemy will be ineffective, as it probably would be in a democracy: you must genuinely intend to retaliate if you are to have any chance of deterring them. You will not want to retaliate if the enemy attacks, because that will have horrendous consequences both for the innocent and for yourself; but you nevertheless want to deter an enemy likely to attack you.

But if retaliation would be evil, isn't it evil to form the intention to retaliate? No doubt, but it might be a lesser evil than risking likely aggression, particularly if enemy aggression was highly probable if undeterred and if it was very unlikely that the threat would have to be carried out. Then if you don't make the threat you will certainly suffer a crippling invasion. In this case those who thought that it was impossible to avoid both evils could claim that you would be justified in choosing the lesser evil.

Of course it may be enough if the enemy, though not fully convinced your threats are sincere, are not confident that you are bluffing either. They might not be prepared to take the risk that you were. But suppose even that would not be enough, that your only hope of deterring their aggression was to make a threat that you truly meant. Then we have the problem that is fancifully illustrated by **The Toxin Paradox** and **The Indy Paradox**: how can you form an intention you know you won't fulfil when it comes to it? One way out of this predicament would be to order less scrupulous people to carry out the retaliation in the event of enemy invasion. But, if you are in a position to order them to do that, you are also in a position to countermand the order before they carry it out. Another way would be to build a Doomsday machine programmed to fire off retaliatory nuclear weapons if the enemy attacked. But what if you couldn't construct a machine that you couldn't demolish or deactivate when the time came?

It would seem that your only recourse would be to try to harden your heart and make yourself more callous, in the hope that you became capable of fulfilling a retaliatory threat and so could form the intention to do so. If the threat fails to deter then it will be irrational to retaliate. So it looks as if we have here a case where it is rational to make yourself less rational. (Cf. **Newcomb's Problem**.) We can only hope that rationality will be regained if the enemy launches its nuclear attack after all.

Gauthier's resolution of **The Toxin Paradox** cannot be applied here – as he recognizes – since you couldn't argue you would be better off if you adopted a policy of making the threat and fulfilling it than if you didn't make the threat in the first place.

None of this is to deny – nor to affirm – that nuclear disarmament would be the safest and most rational policy in the world we actually live in. In making the suppositions above to generate paradox, there is no implicit claim that they are true. But there will probably be less dramatic but actual situations where one evil can only be averted by threatening another and meaning it, and maybe sometimes it will be possible to justify such a threat.

Further Reading

Gregory Kavka, 'Some paradoxes of deterrence', *Journal of Philosophy*, 1978, vol. 75. Kavka also considers some related paradoxes of deterrence.

The Dr Psycho Paradox

Dr Psycho has given you an apple which you have eaten. He may have poisoned it with Z. He offers you a pill which contains X, fatally poisonous by itself but an antidote to Z, though with minor bad side effects. The doctor poisoned the apple if and only if he predicted you were going to take the antidote. He is a good predictor.

So you have a life or death choice: should you take the antidote?

This problem is due to Nicholas Rescher. Rescher produces two conflicting calculations of the expected values of taking and not taking the pill. He takes 1 to be the value of life, -1 the value of death, and 1^- to be the value of life with the bad side effects of the pill. (The superscript minus sign means 'a smidgeon less'.)

In his *Analysis 1* (270–71) he calculates the expected values relative to the correctness of Dr Psycho's prediction, taking p to be the probability that Dr Psycho predicts correctly. If the doctor predicts correctly, you survive; otherwise you die. The expected value of each possible action is the sum of the values of its outcomes weighted by their probabilities:

Expected value of taking the pill = $p(1^-) + (1 - p)(-1) = 2p^- - 1$

Expected value of not taking it = $p(1) + (1 - p)(-1) = 2p - 1$

So the expected value of taking it is less than the expected value of not taking it.

In his *Analysis 2* (271) Rescher calculates the expected values relative to the state of the apple. If p is the probability that the apple was poisoned, then:

Expected value of taking the pill = $p(1^-) + (1 - p)(-1) = 2p^- - 1$

Expected value of not taking = $p(-1) + (1 - p)(1) = -2p + 1$

Now, if $2p^- - 1 > -2p + 1$, as it will if $p > (1/2)^+$, the expected value of taking the pill is greater than that of not taking it. Rescher has added the information that it is (non-trivially) more likely than not that the doctor has poisoned the apple. Because of the discordance between the two analyses in this case he concludes that 'the standard machinery of expected-value analysis may leave us in the lurch because the probabilities may simply fail to be well-defined quantities' (Rescher 2001, 272). For on his view there is nothing to choose between the two analyses.

On *Analysis 1* Rescher assumes that the chance of a correct prediction is the same whether the pill is taken or not (he uses p for both). But if, as he assumes, the chance of the apple's being poisoned exceeds ½, you are more likely to die if you don't take the antidote. But this contradicts his assumption in *Analysis 2* that the state of the apple is independent of whether you take the pill (he uses p for the probability that the pill was poisoned whether you take the antidote or not).

On *Analysis 2*, given that the pill is more likely than not to be poisoned, you are more likely than not to need the antidote to survive. Since you survive if and only if the doctor's prediction is correct, the chance of a correct prediction is greater if you take the pill, which contradicts the assumption in *Analysis 1*.

So the inconsistency lies in the assumptions Rescher sets out with, which undermines his claim that the probabilities are ill-defined and that 'the standard machinery of expected-value analysis has left us in the lurch' (272). He makes a similar mistake in his treatment of Newcomb's Problem.

Since at the point of choice it is already settled whether the apple has been poisoned, it is more appropriate to use what is known as causal decision theory here, what Gibbard and Harper (1978/1981, 156–57) call the 'genuine' expected utility in such cases. 'The "utility of an act"', they say, 'should be its genuine expected efficacy in bringing about states of affairs the agent wants' (168). For Gibbard and Harper, this is to be calculated from the probability of the relevant counterfactuals. So when calculating the expected utility of taking the pill, the relevant probabilities are the probabilities of 'If I were to take the pill I would survive' and 'If I were to take the pill I would not survive'. The probability of the former is plausibly the same as the unconditional probability that the apple has been poisoned, $Pr(P)$, and of the latter that it has not, $1-Pr(P)$. When calculating the utility of not taking the pill, the relevant probabilities are those of 'If I were not to take the pill, I would not survive' and of 'If I were not to take the pill, I would survive'; again, the former is $Pr(P)$ and the latter $1 - Pr(P)$. So this amounts to using Rescher's *Analysis 2* described above, which, to recall, gives us

Expected value of taking the pill = $p(1^-) + (1 - p)(-1) = 2p^- - 1$

Expected value of not taking = $p(-1) + (1 - p)(1) = 1-2p$.

If the apple is more likely to be poisoned than not (by more than a smidgeon), then the rational choice is to take the pill.

Further Reading

Michael Clark and Nicholas Shackel, 'The Dr. Psycho paradox and Newcomb's problem', *Erkenntnis*, 2006, vol. 64, pp. 85–100.
Alan Gibbard and W. L. Harper, 'Counterfactuals and two kinds of expected utility' in C. A. Hooker, J. J. Leach, and E. F. McLennen, eds, *Foundations and Applications of Decision Theory*, Dordrecht, Reidel, 1978. Reprinted in W. L. Harper, R. Stalnaker, and G. Pearce, eds, *Ifs*, Dordrecht, Reidel, 1981, from which page references are taken.
Nicholas Rescher, *Paradoxes*, Chicago and La Salle, Ill., Open Court, 2001, pp. 264–75.

The Eclipse Paradox

During a total solar eclipse we see the moon as a dark round disc silhouetted against the sun. But which side of the moon do we see? Standardly, we do not see an object unless the object causes our perception. But in this case it is the far side of the moon which absorbs and blocks the sunlight from us and causes us to see the moon as a dark disc. So during an eclipse it is the far side of the moon, not its near side, that we see. But that seems quite contrary to the way we think of seeing.

Suppose that you are watching a play and the back of the stage appears to look out on a garden with a tree. Actually there is a large backcloth bearing a photograph lit in such a way that you cannot see from where you are sitting that it is merely a photograph. Furthermore there really is a garden with a tree behind the stage, and if the backcloth and stage wall were not there it would look just the same to you. But in this case you see the backcloth, not the tree in the garden, because your perception is not caused (in the right way) by the tree in the garden. If the photograph is a photograph of that very tree, there is of course *some* causal connection between the tree and your perception, but it is not sufficient to count as your seeing the tree rather than the photograph. This is shown by the fact that it would make no difference if the photograph were of another scene coincidentally indistinguishable from that behind the stage wall: you see the photograph, not the tree.

But does our concept of seeing always require this sort of causal connection? If it does, then we do indeed see the far side of the moon during an eclipse, since the moon appears as a dark disc only because its far side absorbs the sunlight and prevents it reaching us.

Now suppose there are two moons in front of the sun rather than one, and that either of them on its own would cast the same shadow: the near one is smaller and just fits into the conical shadow cast by the far one. It is the far side of the more distant moon which absorbs the sunlight and occludes the sun, and since the near moon is entirely in its shadow the near moon plays no causal part in what we see. Admittedly the near moon would occlude the sun if the far one were not there, but it is there, and as things are it is the far moon which casts the shadow. For an analogy, imagine that a would-be killer, Mac, shoots at his victim but is pre-empted by a marksman who shoots the victim dead before Mac's bullet reaches him. The marksman, not Mac, is the murderer and Mac is merely liable for attempted murder, even though he would have killed had he not been pre-empted.

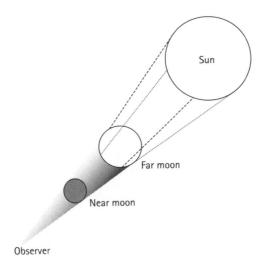

Most of us would be reluctant to say we see the far side of the moon in an eclipse or the (far side of the) far moon in the double eclipse. Is this because we misuse our concept, or is it because the causal connection between object and perception which normally obtains does not hold in every case of seeing? After all, the concept of seeing pre-dates our understanding of the physics of light. Perhaps seeing is a natural kind like gold, and its essence has been revealed at least in part by elucidating the causal mechanisms involved, just as chemists have discovered the chemical essence of gold. But if our ordinary notion of seeing cannot be captured in this way, then there is nothing to stop us from saying that we *do* see the dark nearside of the moon in the single eclipse and the dark nearside of the nearer moon in the double eclipse.

A related puzzle about shadows was discussed at Yale in the late 1960s. (Which moon casts the shadow between the near moon and the observer?) The double eclipse paradox is due to Sorensen.

Further Reading

Roy Sorensen, 'Seeing intersecting eclipses', *Journal of Philosophy*, 1999, vol. 96.

The Paradox of Entailment
(Paradoxes of Strict Implication)

A conclusion follows from, or is *entailed* by, the premisses of an argument just when it is impossible for the premisses to be true and the conclusion false. But a contradiction will entail any conclusion, since it is impossible for a contradiction to be true; a necessary conclusion will be entailed by any premisses, since it is impossible for a necessary conclusion to be false.

This paradox was known in the Middle Ages. It is found, for instance, in the fourteenth-century writings of Pseudo-Scotus, who showed how to derive an arbitrary conclusion from inconsistent premisses. Here is an example:

(1) Pat is both a mother and not a mother
(2) Pat is a mother, from 1
(3) Pat is a mother or Pat is a father, from 2 by the principle of addition

> ('or' here is inclusive, it means 'and/or'. An inclusive 'or' statement, *A* or *B*, is true provided at least one of its disjuncts, *A*, *B*, is true.)

(4) Pat is not a mother, from 1
(5) Pat is a father, from 3, 4, by the principle of disjunctive syllogism.

Any statement whatever can be substituted for the second disjunct of (3) and for (5): 'Paris is the capital of Spain', for example.

Perhaps this is innocuous. *Paris is the capital of Spain* does not intuitively follow from an arbitrary contradiction, but can it not be accepted as a harmless limiting case? After all, no such argument can force us to accept a false conclusion, since we are only obliged to accept the conclusions of those valid arguments whose premisses are true. However, we cannot swallow such entailments without also swallowing those with an arbitrary premiss and a necessary conclusion. And this would mean accepting the entailment of any mathematical theorem by any other.

If these counterintuitive entailments are not to be swallowed, then we must block arguments like that from (1) to (4) above by restricting one of following principles:

(i)   addition: *A* or *B* follows from *A*

(ii) disjunctive syllogism: *B* follows from *A or B*, *not-A*

(iii) the transitivity of entailment, that is, the principle that if *A* entails *B* and *B* entails *C*, then *A* entails *C*.

Each of these three possibilities has been proposed, though in recent years only two have been taken seriously enough to be worked out in great detail, namely restricting (ii) and (iii).

Drop Disjunctive Syllogism

If you reject disjunctive syllogism (or indeed addition) you must restrict transitivity anyway. Consider:

Pat is a mother or (Pat is) a father; Pat is not a mother; so Pat is a father.

(1) Pat is a mother or a father

(2) Pat is not a mother

(3) Pat is a parent, from 1

(4) Pat is a father, from 2, 3.

There won't always be a term like 'parent' to mediate such a transition, but the validity of a logical rule should not depend on a contingent feature like that, on whether a given language happens to have a certain term or phrase. So, unless transitivity is restricted, we will still be able to infer *B* from *A or B* and *not-A*.

There is a similar argument for addition: *Pat is a mother.* So *Pat is a parent.* Hence *Pat is a mother or father.*

Much ingenuity has been exercised in devising relevance logics in which disjunctive syllogism does not hold.

(The formal systems encapsulate a notion of formal entailment, entailments which turn on logical words, like *and*, *or*, and *not*, rather than non-logical words like *parent* and *mother*.)

Drop Transitivity

Neil Tennant has devised a system of logic he calls CR (for *Classical Relevance*), which restricts transitivity in a controlled and allegedly innocuous way, but accepts disjunctive syllogism, and has a certain naturalness. It disallows *A and not-A entails B*, for example, but allows *A and not-A entails A*, because the latter instantiates the unproblematic *A and B entails A*.

It still has *A entails A and (B or not-B)* and *A or (B and not-B) entails A*, however. It is difficult, if not impossible, to formulate satisfactory further restrictions to avoid these. But maybe we could swallow these secondary paradoxes. After all, *A entails A*, and *B or not-B* is a logical truth. *A or (B and not-B) entails A* reflects disjunctive syllogism: as Sherlock Holmes said, 'It's an old maxim of mine that when you have excluded the impossible, whatever remains, however tedious, must be the truth.'

Accept the Classical Definition

But then why not swallow the primary paradoxes? As noted above, there is no danger of drawing false conclusions from acceptable premisses, since inconsistent premisses are never all true. And you will only derive a theorem, T2, from a theorem, T1, if T2 follows without assuming its own theoremhood already. As for inferences with contingent premisses and necessary conclusions, their premisses are redundant, since they are not needed in order to establish the conclusions. But redundant premisses are arguably harmless.

p strictly implies *q* if and only if it is necessary that *if p then q*. So the classical definition of entailment identifies it with strict implication: hence the alternative name 'paradoxes of strict implication'.

Further Reading

Stephen Read, *Thinking about Logic*, Oxford, Oxford University Press, 1995, chapter 2.

*Neil Tennant, *Anti-realism and Logic*, Oxford, Clarendon Press, 1987, chapter 17.

The Paradox of Fiction

We can be afraid of something that does not in fact exist, but it seems we must at least believe it exists. Again, we cannot hate or love anything unless we *believe* it exists. But we also have emotional responses to fiction: we can be afraid of a fictional criminal in a film or feel vengeful when fictional injustice is perpetrated, and in these cases we know the objects of our emotions do not exist.

Does this mean that our emotional responses to fiction are therefore inconsistent or incoherent? Surely not. Failure of emotional response to fiction in many cases betokens insensitivity, which we regard as a defect of character.

It is true that we talk about a 'suspension of disbelief' when engrossed in fiction, and if this suspension were genuine – as perhaps in dreams – the paradox would disappear; while engrossed in a novel, play or film we would temporarily believe in the existence of the fictional characters. But generally we know we are in the cinema or reading a book: we don't jump on to the stage or into the cinema screen to protect a killer's victim, we don't try to tell the police, or send a wreath for the dead victim – not if we are sane, intelligent adults. (Those who send wreaths for characters who die in television soap operas are regarded with amusement.) And features that bring out the artificial nature of the work – the broad brush strokes of impressionist paintings, the high-flown arias of operas – can make the work more, not less, emotionally engaging.

Nor when we react emotionally to fiction do we generally fear thoughts, images or representations. We fear the monster, or at least we fear for characters with whom we identify who are threatened by the monster, and we pity Tolstoy's great fictional creation, Anna Karenina. You can indeed fear thoughts, say obsessive distressing thoughts you are trying to keep at bay. But that is not what is typically happening when we respond to fiction.

And it is not simply a matter of pitying those members of the human race like Anna Karenina, even though the novel may remind us of such human tragedy. Sometimes, admittedly, fiction induces moods in us, with no specific objects: sadness, euphoria, boredom or cynicism, for example. But when we pity Anna Karenina, we don't just feel in a pitying mood, we pity *her*.

On one prominent view fiction is a sort of make-believe, in which we engage as producers or consumers. Pity for Anna Karenina, for example, is construed as a *quasi*-emotion, because it is make-believe. But whereas (unless they are method actors) actors and actresses typically make-believe they are in emotional states without feeling them, spectators feel their responses to fiction and these feelings are not under the control of the will, as make-believe is.

So if we are genuinely afraid of a fictional monster or angry with a fictional cheat why don't we take action as we would in a real case? In non-fictional contexts inclinations to take action may be absent if we know the behaviour is inappropriate in the circumstances, because the object is far in the past or in a distant land, perhaps. There is nothing much we can do in these cases. But our contempt for a past injustice or pity for the plight of distant victims are none the less real. Similarly in fictional cases we don't attempt to intervene when someone is being murdered in a play or film, nor normally do we take evasive action – run from the cinema, call the police – when we fear a fictional object. Yet if emotions directed at past or distant objects are not merely 'quasi-emotions', then why should emotions directed at fictional objects be characterized in this way?

It is true that our fear of a non-fictional object normally subsides if we learn that the object doesn't exist. For example, we were afraid that a hurricane would strike, but now we hear that the hurricane has died down our fear disappears. Nevertheless, when we are involved in fiction, even though we know the objects are fictional, we do have emotional responses to them. In fact, in the fictional case there is an analogue of emotion disappearing with belief in the object. We are afraid the fictional township and inhabitants are going to be hit by a hurricane, but as the story develops it emerges that the hurricane has died out 100 miles away. Typically our fear would disappear.

These considerations suggest that the way to resolve the paradox is simply to recognize fiction as a special case, where we do not need to believe in the existence of objects in order to have emotions towards them.

Some writers can evoke empathy in us for fictional characters who are the sort of person we would normally despise: Gregory Currie has called this 'the paradox of caring'. (See his essay in the collection cited below.) Currie attributes this to imaginative simulation of the character's feelings, but this won't do for cases where, for example, I am afraid or disappointed for a character who doesn't have that emotion because he doesn't yet know that he is in danger or that he has had his hopes dashed. Perhaps our empathy is to be explained by nothing more than the writer's skill in making us see in an understanding and sympathetic light what normally repels us. In any case the phenomenon is not confined to fiction – unpleasant historical characters can be depicted sympathetically too.

See also **The Paradox of Tragedy.**

Further Reading

M. Hjort and S. Laver, eds, *Emotion and the Arts*, Oxford, Oxford University Press, 1997.

Kendall Walton, *Mimesis as Make-believe*, Cambridge, Mass., Harvard University Press, 1990.

The Paradox of Foreknowledge

If God, or indeed anyone, knows that you will get married, how can you be free to marry or not? Foreknowledge of free action seems to be ruled out.

The sentence *If you know you will get married, you must get married* can be interpreted in two different ways. It can be taken as meaning either

(1) It is necessary that (if you know you will get married then you will get married)

or

(2) If you know you will get married then it is necessary that (you will get married).

In the first case we have *necessity of the conditional*: necessarily (if you know that p, then p). In the second, we have *necessity of the consequent* (the 'then' clause): if you know that p, then necessarily p. (1) is true, since you cannot know you will be married if you're not going to be, but (2) doesn't follow from it. On (2), knowledge rules out a future voluntary marriage, whereas on (1) it does not.

But God's omniscience is supposed to be necessary, and the following argument is valid:

(i) Necessarily if God knows you will get married then you will get married

(ii) Necessarily God knows you will get married

So,

(iii) necessarily you will get married.

68

For to say that it is necessary that *if God knows you will get married then you will get married* is to say that you will get married in any possible situation in which God knows you will get married. And to say that *necessarily God knows you will get married* is to say that, in any possible situation, God knows you will get married. So it follows that it is true that you will get married in any possible situation, i.e. that it is necessarily true that you will get married.

However, God's omniscience does not require us to accept the second premiss, (ii), that necessarily God knows you will marry. For God does not know just any old proposition: He will not know you will get married if you are not going to get married. No one, not even God, can know a falsehood. If God is necessarily omniscient, then what is necessary is that *if you will get married then God knows that you will get married.*

But if God, or indeed anyone, already knows that you will marry, it might still seem that you are unable not to marry, for if you failed to marry you would invalidate the knowledge. All that is required, however, is that you marry, and your marrying quite freely will suffice. Similarly, if I know you are reliable then I know you will turn up promptly unless prevented by some event like an unforeseen illness or an accident on the way. But that does not mean that you are forced to be prompt. If you were, then your punctuality would not be a symptom of your reliability.

There remains a problem for the libertarian, though: the libertarian does not believe that determinism is compatible with free will. How then could God invariably know our future actions? He could not predict via deterministic laws, since on the libertarian view our actions are not determined by such laws, so it would seem that backwards causation, from actions to earlier knowledge, would be needed. And there are indeed those who defend the possibility of backward causation.

Boethius (*c.* 480–524) thought that foreknowledge was ruled out, even for God. God doesn't foresee, because He is timeless, and 'beholds as present those future events which happen because of free will'. On this view God sees the whole of history spread out before him in a four-dimensional space-time manifold, and so can be omniscient without threatening our free will. But, if what is said above is right, it is not necessary to rule out foreknowledge in order to make room for free will, unless you are a libertarian.

Although the question, whether foreknowledge of A means that A cannot be a free action, has arisen historically in the context of religious belief in an omniscient God, it is independent of it. We can ask whether it is possible to know of any free act that it will be performed. It is, in any case, questionable whether the notion of omniscience, of *total* knowledge, is consistent: see **The Paradox of Omniscience** and **The Prediction Paradox**.

Further Reading

A. N. Prior, 'The formalities of omniscience', *Philosophy*, 1962, vol. 37.

The Paradox of
Future Generations

In his *Reasons and Persons* (1984) Derek Parfit famously
canvassed what he called 'The Repugnant Conclusion': 'For any
possible population of at least ten billion people, all with a very
high quality of life, there must be some much larger imaginable
population whose existence, if other things are equal, would be
better, even though its members have lives that are barely worth
living' (p. 388).

Parfit is here assuming that the best outcome has 'the greatest
quantity of whatever makes life worth living'. Henry Sidgwick, the
great nineteenth-century utilitarian, had taken a similar view in
terms of happiness; the total not the average was what mattered.
One way of reaching the Repugnant Conclusion involves what
Parfit calls the 'mere addition paradox'. Start with a population (A)
where everyone has a high quality of life. If you add a number of
people with a good but lower quality of life (giving B), you have
greater total well-being. Population C, with the same number as
B, all with the same well-being, has average well-being a little
above that of B but lower than the average in A. C is better than
B (more average well-being and more equality) and B at least as
good as A. Hence C is better than A. By continuing to repeat this
argument (starting with C), we eventually get to a large population,
Z, where each member has very low positive well-being, which
has been shown to be better than A.

The mere addition argument depends on the transitivity of
'better than' (cf. **The Paradox of Preference**), but there is an
alternative form which does not use transitivity. So rejecting
transitivity will not avoid the Repugnant Conclusion.

The *Stanford Encylopedia* article reviews ten ways of dealing with this problem (of which rejecting transitivity is one). These include using the principle of maximizing the *average* well-being instead of the overall maximum, but this is no more successful: as Parfit argues, if Adam and Eve lived marvellous lives, and there are a billion billion other people with lives almost as good as theirs, the average well-being would be lower, and so this population would be worse on that view. No more successful, it seems, are compromise theories according to which the value adding good lives to a population is greater when the original population is smaller. Or the view that improvement comes only if the added life is above a certain critical positive level.

Another approach rejects the Benthamite view that all goods can be measured on a linear scale. Superior goods cannot be compensated for by any amount of the inferior ones. So a world with only inferior goods, 'muzak and potatoes', however large the population, would not be a better one, and the Repugnant Conclusion is avoided. But this approach also has unacceptable consequences. For example, suppose we start with a large population of people whose lives are full of the higher goods. There is a very much larger population where everyone experiences a superior good just once in a lifetime, all the rest being muzak and potatoes; their lives are hardly worth living. Then, the second population is so much larger than the first that its total of superior goods is greater. As Parfit points out (p. 162), it is hard to believe the second world is better.

A further approach involves, for example, only counting the well-being of people actually existing now. That particular view would mean that a small gain for present people would count against a huge loss for future people.

Some have rejected the repugnancy of the conclusion. Even privileged people in the West have lives little different from a population where lives are barely worth living, so this is not so objectionable. True there are desirable features of our lives. In the film *Manhattan* Woody Allen says that what makes *his* life worth living includes Groucho Marx, Willie Mays, the second movement of the *Jupiter Symphony*, Louis Armstrong's *Potato Head Blues*, Swedish movies, Flaubert's *Sentimental Education*, Marlon Brando, Frank Sinatra, and Cézanne's picture of apples and pears. On the other hand most of us experience countervailing miseries: toothache, bereavement, illness, depression, injury, disappointment, personal animosity, burglary, and so on. One trouble with this view is that there is a much larger population, where each person has such a tiny surplus of what is worthwhile over their miseries, that life really is barely worth living at all, but with a greater total well-being, and that is undeniably repugnant.

It looks as if philosophers are still searching for a solution to this problem. Perhaps, as some have argued, there can be no satisfactory population ethics.

Further Reading

Gustaf Arrhenius, Jesper Ryberg and Torbjörn Tännsjö, 'The repugnant conclusion' in *The Stanford Encyclopedia of Philosophy* (Fall 2010 edition), ed. Edward N. Zalta, http://plato.stanford.edu/archives/fall2010/entries/repugnant-conclusion/.

Derek Parfit, *Reasons and Persons*, Part 4, Oxford, Oxford University Press, 1984.

Derek Parfit, 'Overpopulation and the quality of life', in P. Singer, ed., *Applied Ethics*, Oxford, Oxford University Press, 1986.

Henry Sidgwick, *The Methods of Ethics*, 6th edn, London, Macmillan, 1901, pp. 415–16.

Galileo's Paradox

On the face of it there would seem to be more whole numbers (1, 2, 3, . . .) than squares of those numbers (1, 4, 9, . . .).

But the whole numbers can be paired off with their squares:

1	2	3	4	5	6	7	8	. . .
↕	↕	↕	↕	↕	↕	↕	↕	
1	4	9	16	25	36	49	64	. . .

and so there are just as many of one as the other.

The squares of numbers seem to be far fewer than all the positive whole numbers (the integers), and if you pick them out from the sequence of integers arranged in their usual ascending order they rapidly thin out. Yet, as the incredulous Galileo (1564–1642) noticed, they can be exhaustively paired off with all the positive integers: each positive integer has a unique square associated with it and each square has a unique positive integer (its positive square root) associated with it. The squares form what is called a *proper subset* of the positive integers, that is a subset whose membership falls short of the set of positive integers, and is therefore distinct from it. Yet the subset can be mapped without remainder onto the set of all the positive integers. So are there fewer squares or just as many?

We are so accustomed to thinking of finite collections that our intuitions become disturbed when we first consider infinite sets like the set of positive integers. Consider first how we count finite sets. Suppose that there are two piles, one of red balls, the other of blue, and you wish to determine which, if either, is more numerous. The most straightforward way would be to pair off the red balls with the blue ones and see whether either colour was exhausted before the other: if you could pair them off one-to-one without remainder then you could conclude that there were just as many red balls as blue ones, that the piles were equinumerous. Obviously if there were any unmatched blue balls then you would conclude that there were more blue balls than red. That two sets have the same number when the members of one correspond one-to-one with the members of the other is an idea which is fundamental to our practice of counting and our notion of number. David Hume (1710–76) knew this: 'When two numbers are so combin'd, as that the one has always an unit corresponding to every unit of the other, we pronounce them equal.' Counting the balls in each pile, and comparing the results, implicitly involves such one-to-one matching. You match each of the red balls with a different one of the first 423 whole numbers, say, and if you can do the same with the blue balls without remainder you conclude the piles are equinumerous. This is justified because if the red balls pair off with the first 423 integers, and the first 423 integers pair off with the blue balls, the red balls must pair off with the blue ones. Of course, you would normally use the integers in their natural ascending order, starting with 1 and ending with 423, especially if you did not know the number of balls in each pile to start with. But it would be sufficient for establishing equinumerosity that you could pair off the red and blue balls respectively with the first 423 integers taken *in any order*.

Counting Infinite Sets

When we come to counting infinite sets we need to generalize the notion of whole number to that of cardinal number. You obviously cannot answer questions like *How many even numbers are there?* and *How many prime numbers are there?* by giving a positive whole number. Those cardinal numbers which number infinite sets are known as *transfinite*. Their arithmetic was worked out by Cantor, and turns out to have some very peculiar features.

We saw that two finite sets were equinumerous if and only if their members could be paired off one-to-one without remainder. The order in which the members of one set are paired off with those of the other does not matter. For example, take the sets {Tom, Dick} and {Jill, Mary}. You can pair off Tom with Jill and Dick with Mary; or you can pair off Tom with Mary and Dick with Jill. Either pairing is sufficient to establish that the sets have the same number. When you pair off the blue balls with the red ones, the order in which you take the balls is immaterial. Piaget tells of a mathematician who chose his career because of a childhood flash of inspiration while counting some stones. He counted them from left to right and found there were ten, and then he counted them from right to left with the same result. 'Then he put them in a circle and, finding ten again, he was very excited. He found, essentially, that the sum is independent of the order.'

It does not need much reflection to see that, whenever members of a finite set can be paired off in one order with members of another, they can be paired off in any other order. But this does not apply to infinite sets. Consider the sequence of positive integers in which all the odd numbers, in their natural ascending order, precede all the even numbers:

1, 3, 5, 7, 9, 11, . . . , 2, 4, 6, 8, 10, 12, . . .

and compare it with the sequence of all the positive integers in ascending order:

1, 2, 3, 4, 5, 6, . . .

If you now imagine the members of the first sequence paired off, in the order given, with the members of the second sequence, in their order, you will see that the odd numbers in the first sequence exhaust all the members of the second sequence, which therefore has nothing left to pair with the first sequence's even numbers.

1, 3, 5, 7, 9, 11, ..., 2, 4, 6, 8, 10, 12, ...

↕ ↕ ↕ ↕ ↕ ↕

1, 2, 3, 4, 5, 6, ...

Every number from the second sequence gets matched with an odd number in the first sequence. 2 gets matched with 3, and in general a number in the lower sequence gets matched with one less than its double. In short, the whole numbers cannot be paired off with themselves if they are taken in the orders of the two sequences above.

There seem to be two non-arbitrary ways of generalizing the notion of number to accommodate infinite sets. We could say that infinite sets are equinumerous if and only if their respective members can be paired off in at least one order; or we could say that they are equinumerous if and only if they can be paired off in every possible order. But the second way is obviously too stringent, since, if we chose that, we should have to deny that the set of whole numbers was equinumerous with itself. We are left with the first proposal, which emerges as the only feasible one. So a set x has the same cardinal number as a set y if and only if there is *some* one-to-one correspondence between the members of x and the members of y.

In the case of the finite piles of balls we saw that there were more blue balls if the red balls paired off exhaustively with only some of the blue ones. In the case of finite sets we can say that a set x is larger than a set y if and only if y is equinumerous with a *proper* subset of x. But this does not work with infinite sets, as Galileo's pairing shows. There are just as many squares of positive integers as there are positive integers. In general, x is larger than *or equal* in size (cardinality) to y if and only if y is equinumerous with a subset of x.

A set whose members can be paired off one-to-one with the positive integers is said to be *denumerable*. A set is *countable* if and only if it is either finite or denumerably infinite.

Galileo's Paradox

An infinite set is now *defined* as 'Dedekind-infinite' if it can be mapped onto a proper subset of itself, after J. W. R. Dedekind (1831–1916). (Given the axiom of choice – see note below – it can be shown that all infinite sets are Dedekind-infinite.) The point behind Galileo's paradox was noticed as early as Plutarch (*c.* 46–120). Proclus, the fifth-century commentator on Euclid, remarked that a circle has infinitely many different diameters and that, since each diameter divides the circle into two, there is apparently a double infinity of halves. It is evident that the double infinity can be mapped onto one of the single infinities: interleaving the two will give a single enumeration.

Note on the Axiom of Choice

The axiom of choice, mentioned parenthetically in the last paragraph, is an axiom of set theory which is actually presupposed in the proof of the theorem given in the entry on Cantor's paradox. It states that, if you have a – possibly infinite – set of non-empty sets, then there is a set with just one member chosen from each of them.

See also **Hilbert's Hotel, The Tristram Shandy, Cantor's Paradox.**

Further Reading

A. W. Moore, *The Infinite*, 2nd edn, London and New York, Routledge, 2001, chapters 1 and 8.

The Gentle Murder Paradox
(The Good Samaritan)

If you commit murder you ought to do so gently. Suppose then that you do commit murder. Then you ought to do so gently. Now from *you ought to do A* it follows that you ought to do anything logically implied by A. (For example, from *I ought to help my mother and spend time with my children* it follows that *I ought to help my mother*.) *You are murdering gently* entails *you are committing murder*. So it follows that *you ought to commit murder*.

This is a version, due to J. W. Forrester, of the paradox known as 'the Good Samaritan'.

You ought not to commit murder. So, by the argument above, it follows that if you commit murder, you both ought and ought not to do so. Now there may indeed be cases where you both ought and ought not to do something, as when I promise to take my daughter to a party and my son to a film. The party was to be today, the film tomorrow, but both events are then postponed until 3 o'clock the day after tomorrow, so that I cannot keep both promises. I have conflicting obligations, both genuine. (See **The Paradox of Democracy**.) But the 'ought and ought not' in the murder example is not a case of conflicting obligations like these. So something must be wrong with the argument.

There is a case for challenging the inference from 'If you commit murder then you ought to commit murder gently' and 'You are committing murder' to 'You ought to commit murder gently' . If the scope of the 'ought' is the whole conditional rather than simply the 'then' clause, the conclusion does not follow.

It ought to be the case that (if you commit murder then you do so gently).

You are committing murder.

do not logically imply that you ought to commit murder gently.

But even if the 'ought' has narrow scope and the inference goes through, we can question the general principle that when you ought to do A you ought to do anything entailed (logically implied) by A. 'You ought to confess your sins' entails that you have sinned, but surely not that you ought to have done so.

Indeed, when we see how analogous principles fail, it ceases to have any attraction. Consider:

'I'm glad you corrected your mistakes'

from which it does not follow that I'm glad you made mistakes, even though you cannot correct your mistakes if you haven't made any.

'She wants to grow old gracefully'

from which it does not follow that she wants to grow old, even though you cannot grow old gracefully if you do not grow old.

'I'm sorry you missed our wedding'

from which it does not follow that I'm sorry our wedding took place, even though you cannot miss a wedding if it didn't take place.

Further Reading

J. W. Forrester, 'Gentle murder and the adverbial Samaritan', *Journal of Philosophy*, 1984, vol. 81. For the original Good Samaritan version see P. H. Nowell-Smith and E. J. Lemmon, 'Escapism: the logical basis of ethics', *Mind*, 1960, vol. 69.

The Paradox of the Gods

A man wants to walk a mile from a point *a*. But there is an infinity of gods each of whom, unknown to the others, intends to obstruct him. One of them will raise a barrier to stop his further advance if he reaches the half-mile point, a second if he reaches the quarter-mile point, a third if he goes one-eighth of a mile, and so on ad infinitum. So he cannot even get started, because however short a distance he travels he will already have been stopped by a barrier. But in that case no barrier will rise, so that there is nothing to stop him setting off. He has been forced to stay where he is by the mere unfulfilled intentions of the gods.

Of course our own world does not contain such gods, but it seems possible in principle – it's not excluded by logic – that all of the gods could form their intentions and set in place a comprehensive system of obstruction. This however is an illusion. Imagine that the gods lay mines along the route which will ensure that a barrier rises at a point if the man reaches that point. The system cannot survive being tested. For if the man gets away from *a*, however little distance he goes, a barrier will have risen to obstruct him before he gets there. A barrier is supposed to rise at a point *p* if and only if the man gets to *p*, and so if and only if no barrier has risen before *p*.

There is no first point beyond *a* at which a barrier can rise. The sequence of points

$$\ldots, \; {}^{1}/_{64}, \; {}^{1}/_{32}, \; {}^{1}/_{16}, \; {}^{1}/_{8}, \; {}^{1}/_{4}, \; {}^{1}/_{2}$$

has an end but no beginning. If there were a first point in this sequence then the man could get there before being obstructed. But any point on the route from *a* at which one of the gods intends to raise a barrier will be preceded by infinitely many points at each of which some god intends to raise a barrier if the man reaches it. The system of obstruction as a whole will not work as intended: if the man gets going, not all their intentions can be fulfilled. Recall that, in effect, each god intends to raise a barrier at his point if and only if no barrier nearer a has already been raised. For suppose the man gets going. Either at least one barrier rises, or no barriers go up at all. If a barrier rises, a god will have raised it despite the existence of barriers nearer a; if there is no point at which a barrier rises, each god will have refrained from raising his barrier even though there is no preceding barrier. So the set-up is logically flawed. And, once we see that, the puzzle disappears.

The paradox was invented by J. Benardete. See pp. 259–60 of his book *Infinity* (Oxford: Clarendon Press, 1964). The resolution given above is drawn from the paper by Stephen Yablo cited below.

See also **Yablo's Paradox.**

Further Reading

Jon Pérez Laraudogoitia, 'Priest on the paradox of the gods', *Analysis*, 2000, vol. 60.

Graham Priest, 'On a version of one of Zeno's paradoxes', *Analysis* 1999, vol. 59.

Stephen Yablo, 'A reply to new Zeno', *Analysis*, 2000, vol. 60.

Grue (Goodman's 'New Riddle of Induction')

If we generalize on the basis of emeralds we have examined we can reach the conclusion that all emeralds are green. Now define a new adjective, 'grue': x is grue if it is green and examined (by now), or blue and unexamined (by now). If we generalize on the basis of previously examined emeralds it seems we can also reach the contrary conclusion that all emeralds are grue.

Not only are all examined emeralds green, they are also, because already examined, grue. The unexamined emeralds cannot be both green and grue, since if they are grue and unexamined they are blue. If it is licit to argue from *All examined emeralds are green* to *All emeralds are green*, why is it illicit to argue to *All emeralds are grue*?

The property *grue* looks suspicious and gerrymandered, and apparently less fundamental than blue or green. But if we had the concepts of grue and of bleen (blue if examined, green if not) first, then we could define green and blue in terms of *them*. Green, for example, would be defined as grue if examined and bleen if not. We can also imagine circumstances in which we would have a use for 'grue'. Suppose there were a sort of precious stone which was sensitive to examination (which we will assume is a matter of looking at the stone) and when exposed to light changed from blue to green. We may suppose that exposure to light produces a chemical change, which if it could have been inhibited would have left the gems looking blue. Then all of these stones would be grue, not just the examined ones.

We do not believe emeralds are like that, however. Scientists know about their physical structure, and know stones with this structure do not turn from blue to green on exposure to light. We therefore have good reason to believe that if an unexamined emerald had been examined it would have been green and would not have changed colour, so we do not believe that unexamined emeralds are grue. The examined emeralds count as grue only because they have been examined, and our background knowledge tells us that being examined doesn't change them from blue to green. If they are green when examined then they were green, not grue, before. In short, we cannot generalize in a simple way from cases we have examined to all other cases, without relevant background information. We can properly make the generalization only if that background information entitles us to regard the examined cases as a representative sample with respect to the property in question. The imagined stones which lost their blue colour when exposed to light were not a representative sample with respect to green, since the sample included none of those yet unexposed to light. That they have been examined, however, does not rule out the emeralds as a representative sample for green as opposed to grue, since we know that the normal examination of emeralds has no physical or chemical effect on them.

If our background information includes the fact that a certain feature of our sample biases it with respect to the property in question, then generalization is certainly illicit. For example, if a survey of university students finds that more of them vote for the left than the right, it is obviously wrong to conclude that this is true of the general population, since we know how age affects voting patterns. And even if we did not know how age affects voting patterns, given what else we know about differences in attitude between the younger and older generations, we could not assume that voting patterns would be the same in young and old. Enumerative induction, the mere accumulation of positive instances of a generalization, is worthless on its own (as the discussion of **The Paradox of the Ravens** also illustrates).

What if we started with *grue* and defined 'green' as 'grue and examined' and 'blue' as 'grue and unexamined'? Now the emeralds we have examined are grue and green. What of the unexamined ones? Well, it is a feature of grue things that they are blue if unexamined. Our sample is unrepresentative for grue since it contains only examined gems.

If there is nothing in our background information to help us determine whether examined cases are typical, then we should refrain from making any generalizations until we have done more investigation, so that we acquire an idea of what factors might skew our sample.

Though anticipated by Russell, the paradox is principally associated with Nelson Goodman, who published a version of it in 1946 – his example of *grue* came later. The word 'gruebleen' had appeared in James Joyce's *Finnegans Wake* (1939).

Further Reading

Nelson Goodman, *Fact, Fiction and Forecast*, Cambridge, Mass., Harvard University Press, 1955; 4th edn, Cambridge, Mass., Harvard University Press, 1983.

R. M. Sainsbury, *Paradoxes*, 3rd edn, Cambridge, Cambridge University Press, 2009, pp. 99–107.

Douglas Stalker, ed., *Grue! the New Riddle of Induction*, Chicago, Open Court, 1994. Fifteen papers with an extensive annotated bibliography covering 316 publications. According to the introduction there are now about twenty different approaches to the problem.

Alan Weir, 'Gruesome perceptual spaces', *Analysis*, 1995, vol. 55, for a stronger version of the paradox, which he argues cannot be dealt with so easily.

The Heap (The Bald Man, The Sorites, Little-by-little Arguments)

10,000 grains suitably arranged make a heap. But, at no point can you convert a collection of grains that is a heap into one that is not, simply by removing a single grain. So it follows that a single grain makes a heap. For if we keep removing grains over and over again, say 9,999 times, at no point does it cease to be a heap. Yet we obviously know that a single grain is not a heap.

Let us set out the argument above more explicitly.

Argument I

A pile of 10,000 grains is a heap.
If 10,000 grains are a heap, so are 9,999 grains.
So 9,999 grains are a heap.
If 9,999 grains are a heap, so are 9,998 grains.
So 9,998 grains are a heap.

$$\vdots$$
$$\vdots$$

If 2 grains are a heap, so is one grain.
So one grain is a heap.

The conclusion is reached here by repeated applications of the logical form of inference known as *modus ponens* (or *affirming the antecedent*): if p then q; p; so q. This sort of chain argument, in which the conclusion of each sub-argument becomes a premiss of the next, is called a 'sorites'.

The argument can be formulated more compactly in the following way, in which the 'if' premisses of Argument I are generalized in the second premiss of Argument II:

Argument II

A pile of 10,000 grains is a heap.
For any number n greater than 1, if a pile of n grains is a heap then so is a pile of $n - 1$ grains.
So one grain is a heap.

The premiss could contain any arbitrarily large number without affecting the apparent validity of the argument. The premisses appear indisputable but the conclusion is obviously false.

Compare Argument II with this argument about temperature:

A temperature of 60°F is above freezing point.
For any (whole number) n, if n°F is above freezing point, then so is a temperature of $(n-1)$°F .
So a temperature of 1°F is above freezing point.

The second premiss is false because of the sharp cut-off point at 32°F. But there does not seem to be any point at which the subtraction of a single grain can make all the difference between a heap and a non-heap. Gradually the subtraction of grains will make it cease to be a heap, but there seems to be no clean point of transition. Unless we are to retreat to scepticism about the existence of any objects whose terms are vague, we must find a reason for rejecting Arguments I and II.

Our language seems to contain many vague nouns and adjectives which could be used to construct sorites arguments like those above. Obvious examples are 'adult', 'book', 'mountain', 'lake', 'hot', 'bald', 'heavy' and 'tall'. The child, for example, grows into an adult after the passage of many millions of seconds. It would seem absurd to think that there is a child at one moment and an adult a second later. By contrast, attaining the legal age of majority is achieved overnight at a precise time.

Epistemic View

Yet there have been both ancient and modern philosophers who have denied gradual transitions where vague terms are involved, claiming that one of the premises of the sorites argument is straightforwardly false. There *is* a sharp cut-off point, it is just that we do not know where it is. The adjective 'epistemic' ('pertaining to knowledge') is applied to this view, since it treats our failure to detect a sharp transition as merely a defect in our knowledge. This is simply because our powers of discrimination are limited and we have to recognize margins of error. For example, suppose we are looking at a spectrum of shades of colour on which red gradually turns to purple. If there were a definite point which marked the end of the red section, we should not be able to discriminate shades just either side of that point which were none the less distinct. Similarly, if an accumulation of grains organized and configured in a certain way became a heap as soon as it had a certain number of grains, a pile with one grain fewer would ordinarily look no different to us. Our beliefs here are not reliable and so do not constitute knowledge.

But at most this explains why we cannot detect cut-off points. It does not show that there really is a cut-off point between shades and between heaps and non-heaps. We may not be able to detect the exact cut-off point between 32°F and less than 32°F when the temperature falls below freezing point – there are margins of error even in our use of precision instruments – but we know what it is and what we are trying to detect.

In many cases it is difficult to see how we could acquire precise notions without first having vague ones. If we did not have adjectives like 'hot', how could we acquire the notion of temperature? Two objects have the same temperature if one is just as hot as the other. Children don't learn what temperature is first and *then* come to understand the word 'hot'.

Nevertheless, these considerations are probably not decisive. The epistemic view has distinguished contemporary proponents, who have deployed considerable ingenuity in its defence.

Degrees of Truth

If there is a genuine borderline between heaps and non-heaps, then a statement that says of a borderline case that it is a heap is not strictly true, but it *is* roughly true. Is France hexagonal? Not exactly, but it is roughly true that it is. Olivia is 5′ 7″. Is it true to say she is tall? Only roughly. But if she grows another inch the claim is closer to the truth. This suggests that there are degrees of truth. Some borderline heaps are closer to being heaps than others: the attribution of the term 'heap' becomes less accurate as more grains are subtracted, until there are so few that it becomes unequivocally false. Even the subtraction of a single grain brings the accumulation slightly closer to being a non-heap, though the difference is so tiny that it will rarely concern us. Admittedly, the falling winter temperature will get closer and closer to freezing point as it goes down, but it is strictly true that it is not below freezing point before it goes below 32°F, and as soon as it does the statement that it is below freezing point is strictly true.

Suppose we are within the borderline for a heap when there are 70 grains, and consider the conditional statement

If 71 grains make a heap, then so do 70.

Both the 'if' part (the antecedent), '71 grains make a heap', and the 'then' part (the consequent), '70 grains make a heap', are, taken on their own, roughly true, but 71 grains are closer to being a heap than 70, so the antecedent is nearer the truth than the consequent. Now a conditional is clearly false if its antecedent is true and consequent false, as is the case, for example, with 'If New Orleans is the largest city in Louisiana, it is the state capital'. So if we recognize that there can be degrees of truth, it seems reasonable to say that a conditional whose antecedent is closer to the truth than its consequent falls short of being strictly true. It may not fall very short. It may fall short only to a very tiny degree. But that is enough to stop the sorites argument being sound, for not all its premises will be strictly true. Quite a few of the 9,999 conditional premises in Argument I above will deviate very slightly from the truth. These tiny errors propagate through the chain to yield a wholly erroneous conclusion, as surely as the continued subtraction of grains destroys a heap. Similarly the generalization in the second premiss of Argument I ('For any number n greater than 1, if a pile of n grains is a heap then so is a pile of $n - 1$ grains') will fall short of the truth by a significant degree, because many of its instances fall short.

Various attempts have been made to provide logics which assign precise numerical degrees of truth to statements. But often such assignments are quite artificial. What value should you assign to 'France is hexagonal'? It would have to be less than 1 and presumably greater than 0.5, but any assignment within this range would seem to be quite arbitrary. How could you possibly decide whether 'The Middle Ages ended in 1485' should be assigned a higher or lower value than the statement about the shape of France?

Even if we are prepared to accept this artificiality, the logics used tend to have counterintuitive consequences. So-called fuzzy logic is a popular choice. A common version gives a conjunctive statement the same value as that of its lowest conjunct. For example, if 'Amanda is tall' is assigned 0.8 and 'Sam is tall' is assigned 0.95, then the conjunction 'Amanda is tall and Sam is tall' gets the value 0.8. This may seem reasonable enough. But suppose we have a conjunction of six conjuncts each of which gives the population of a specified area. Each of the first five gives the population of a large country and is 99 per cent accurate, but the last says that the population of the little town of Uzès is 3,000 when it is actually 3,750. Presumably the last conjunct would have a degree of truth of about 0.8, which would be inherited, with questionable justice, by the whole conjunction. Worse, if Amanda is borderline tall so that 'Amanda is tall' is assigned 0.5, the necessary falsehood 'Amanda is tall and not tall' gets the value 0.5.

A more serious problem for the use of these logics, however, is that they do not dispense with sharp transitions. They accommodate the gradual transition from heap to non-heap at the expense of imposing a sharp transition from heap to borderline, and from borderline to non-heap. For among the conditional premisses of Argument I there will be a first and a last that falls short of 1. This is known as the problem of higher-order vagueness.

	↓		↓
— heaps —	— borderline cases —	— not heaps —

Supervaluations

So it looks as if we should avoid assigning precise numerical values as degrees of truth. To assign ranges of values will not help either. But roughly true statements must somehow be distinguished from those which are strictly true. Another approach is to treat them as neither true nor false, and identify them as those which could become true or false by admissible ways of making the vague term precise. For scientific and legal purposes we often need a precise term, and one way of introducing it is to tighten up an existing vague one. For example, although the transition from childhood is normally a very gradual one, the law needs a precise cut-off point after which the legal duties and rights of adults can be assigned to citizens. The term 'child' could be made precise in a number of admissible ways: 'under age 16' and 'under age 21' are all right, but it would violate the sense of the term to sharpen it to 'under the age of two', or 'under the age of 65'. 'A person aged six is a child' is true under all admissible sharpenings ('supertrue'). 'Someone aged 60 is a child' is false under all admissible sharpenings ('superfalse'). But 'Someone aged 16 is a child' would be true under some sharpenings, false under others, and so count as neither supertrue nor superfalse. So we have three possible values: supertrue, superfalse, and neither. These are known as *supervaluations*, and their formal properties have been worked out in detail with considerable elegance. Arguments I and II again fail to be sound because not all their premisses will be (super)true. The approach also avoids the counterintuitive consequences that can arise when fuzzy logic is employed to handle vagueness.

But it still fails to solve the problem of higher-order vagueness. In Argument II, for example, there will be a first premiss which is neither true nor false, and a last one: the borderline is again sharply delimited. And elaboration of the logic to avoid this has been found to introduce other counterintuitive consequences.

The three approaches sketched above do not exhaust the solutions that have been mooted, but they are currently the most prominent.

Perhaps a 'degree of truth' view can be rescued if we refrain from interpreting it in terms of some system of logic. It will have to recognize that it is indeterminate where the borderline begins and ends, in such a way that it doesn't follow that there is a determinate range of cases where it is indeterminate whether they are on the borderline – or a determinate range of cases where it is indeterminate whether it is indeterminate that they are on the borderline, and so on. One way of doing this has been suggested by Oswald Hanfling (see the paper cited below): borderline cases are those which we hesitate to classify, but the point at which we start to hesitate will typically vary from time to time and person to person.

The paradox has been traced back to Eubulides, a contemporary of Aristotle.

See also **Quinn's Paradox, Wang's Paradox.**

Further Reading

Patrick Grim, 'The buried quantifier: an account of vagueness and the sorites', *Analysis*, 2005, vol. 65.

Oswald Hanfling, 'What is wrong with sorites arguments?', *Analysis*, 2001, vol. 61.

Rosanna Keefe, *Theories of Vagueness*, Cambridge, Cambridge University Press, 2000.

Rosanna Keefe and Peter Smith, eds, *Vagueness: A Reader*, Cambridge, Mass. and London, MIT Press, 1987. Contains an excellent introductory survey and a range of important papers.

R. M. Sainsbury, *Paradoxes*, 3rd edn, Cambridge, Cambridge University Press, 2009, chapter 3.

R. M. Sainsbury and Timothy Williamson, 'Sorites', chapter 18 in R. Hale and C. Wright, eds, *A Companion to the Philosophy of Language*, Oxford, Blackwell, 1997.

Roy Sorensen, *Vagueness and Contradiction*, Oxford, Oxford University Press, 2001.

Timothy Williamson, *Vagueness*, London, Routledge, 1994.

Heraclitus' Paradox

As Heraclitus said, you cannot step into the same river twice.

For, if Heraclitus had bathed in a river on Saturday and the same river on Sunday, he would have bathed in the same water on the two successive days, since whatever is a river is water. But it wouldn't have been the same water, so it wouldn't have been the same river.

We are to suppose, of course, that the river is flowing, so that the water Heraclitus bathes in on Saturday cannot be the same water he bathes in on Sunday. But since we know that it is perfectly possible to bathe in the same flowing river on successive days, we need to find a way of blocking the inference.

Is what he bathes in on successive days the same or different? It is surely perverse to force an answer to this question without a further gloss. To someone who puts this question, shouldn't we ask whether she means the same river or the same water? According to what is known as the doctrine of relative identity, there is no such thing as simple identity: to say that a is the same as b is to say something incomplete. a must be the same river, the same water, the same word, the same colour, as b; it can't simply be the same, full stop. It is a consequence of this position that a can be the same F as b but a different G. For example, on the line below

(1) cat   (2) cat

(1) is the same type-word as (2), but they are different token-words. A book may be the same novel but a different translation.

Call the river r. Let the water in r at the time Heraclitus steps into the river on Saturday be $w_{SATURDAY}$, and the water in r at the time he steps into the river on Sunday be w_{SUNDAY}. On the relative identity view, on Saturday r is the same water as $w_{SATURDAY}$, on Sunday the same water as w_{SUNDAY}. Although $w_{SATURDAY}$ is not the same water as w_{SUNDAY}, it is – on the relative identity view – the same river. So Heraclitus steps into the same river on successive days but into different water. This blocks the paradoxical inference, but has its problems. Clearly the life histories of r, $w_{SATURDAY}$ and w_{SUNDAY} are different. For example, the volume of water $w_{SATURDAY}$ will eventually mingle with the sea and cease to belong to the river. But if r is identified with $w_{SATURDAY}$, as it would be on Saturday, how could this be? Wouldn't whatever was true of $w_{SATURDAY}$ be true of r? Yet the locations of r and $w_{SATURDAY}$ are different at other times. Contrast Lewis Carroll, who was the same man as Rev. C. L. Dodgson, and who therefore had precisely the same life history as C. L. Dodgson. It is true that before he adopted the pen-name he was known only as 'Dodgson', but it was the same man whose original name was 'Dodgson' who came to be known as 'Carroll', and who had just one life-history, whatever he was called on different occasions.

Nevertheless, it may still seem that the river is identical with a volume of water like $w_{SATURDAY}$ at a particular time. Now, if you bathe in the river at one location and then at another, you bathe in the same river by bathing in different spatial parts of it. On another conception currently popular among philosophers the river is a sequence of temporal parts, or time-slices; it has four dimensions, three spatial, and one temporal. On this view, if you bathed in the river on successive days, you would be bathing in the same river by bathing in different temporal parts of it, just as you can bathe in the same river by bathing in different spatial parts of it. The different temporal parts could be identified with different, but related, volumes of water. However, the four-dimensional view has a problem too. The river is something which changes, and change seems to require a persistent substance which changes. If we merely had a sequence of temporal parts, a sequence of related volumes of water, what would change?

Whether anything can be made of the four-dimensional view, the relation between the river r and the volumes of water $w_{SATURDAY}$ and w_{SUNDAY} is better regarded as one of composition than of identity. When we say that brass is copper and zinc, we are not saying that brass is identical with copper and zinc, we are saying what brass is composed of. If we ask whether the table-top is wood or plastic, we are not asking about its identity but about its composition. Equally, when we ask whether the statue is marble or stone, we are asking what the statue is made of. The river is made up of a volume of water, and of different volumes of water at different times. That is how it can change, how it flows. So the second premiss ('Whatever is a river is water') is true only if it construed as meaning that rivers are made up of water; and they are not normally made up of the same volume of water throughout their history. On this construal, then, we can infer only that Heraclitus stepped into something made up of water on each day, without the implication that the water was the same on both occasions.

See also **The Paradox of the Many, The Ship of Theseus.**

Further Reading

David Wiggins, *Sameness and Substance Renewed*, Cambridge, Cambridge University Press, 2001, chapter 1.

Heterological (Grelling's Paradox, The Grelling–Nelson Paradox)

A predicate expression is *heterological* if and only if it doesn't apply to itself, *autological* if and only if it does. For example, 'is monosyllabic', 'is a French phrase', and 'is three words long' are heterological, since they don't apply to themselves, whereas 'is polysyllabic', 'is an English phrase', and 'is four words long' are autological.

Is 'is heterological' heterological? If it is heterological, it doesn't apply to itself and so it is not. If it is not, it does apply to itself, and so is heterological. In other words, it is if and only if it isn't.

(1a) One solution is to treat predicates about predicates as one level higher than their subjects, so that a statement about a predicate is only accepted as significant if its predicate is of a level one higher than that of its subject. So 'short' cannot apply to itself, since both subject and predicate in *'Short' is short* would be of the same level. *'Heterological' is heterological* will also be disqualified for the same reason, as will *'Heterological' is autological*. No predicate can properly be applied to or denied of itself: a predicate can only properly be applied to a predicate one level lower, and therefore distinct from itself. On this view, the question whether 'heterological' is heterological or autological cannot properly be raised. The very question is excluded by the rule about levels, and so the paradox does not arise. But it is highly counterintuitive to dismiss as meaningless the statements that 'short' is short and that 'monosyllabic' is not monosyllabic. The distinction of levels when predicates are applied to predicates seems simply gerrymandered to avoid the present paradox.

(1b) An alternative solution is to recognize a hierarchy of 'heterological's and 'autological's. Call 'heterological$_2$' a second-level predicate which is true of first-level predicates which don't apply to themselves. 'Heterological$_3$' is true only of first- and second-level predicates, and is itself a third-level predicate. And so on. This hierarchy differs from that in (1a) in allowing predicates – except these 'heterological's (and the correlative 'autological's) – to apply to themselves. The exception means that there will be no 'heterological$_i$' which applies to all levels including level i. So once again paradox is avoided. But it is more simply avoided by having a single typeless adjective 'heterological' which is undefined for itself as subject. Which leads us to (2).

(2) A better resolution parallels one suggested for **The Liar** (proposal 3), but without the restriction to tokens: *'heterological' is heterological* is neither true nor false, since it is not a statement with any genuine content. When we consider whether it is true that 'monosyllabic' is monosyllabic, we look at the number of syllables in the expression and see that it isn't. But we cannot tell from the expressions 'heterological', 'autological' whether or not they apply to themselves. In order to know whether 'is heterological' is heterological we need to know whether it applies to itself, that is, we need to know the answer to our question before we can answer it! (Compare analogous diagnoses of the paradoxes of **Validity, Berry, Richard, Russell, The Liar** and **Curry**.) But we can still say that 'short' is autological because 'short' is short, and that 'monosyllabic' is heterological because it is not monosyllabic.

(3) Yet another solution appeals to dialetheism, according to which we can accept the contradiction that 'heterological' is both heterological and autological. But we disregard that possibility here, as we do below in the discussion of **The Liar** (q.v. for an explanation of dialetheism).

The paradox originated in an article in German by K. Grelling and L. Nelson, 'Remarks on the paradoxes of Russell and Burali–Forti' (1908). A variant appeared in Russell's *Principles of Mathematics* (1903).

Further Reading

Robert L. Martin, 'On Grelling's paradox', *Philosophical Review*, 1968, vol. 77.

Hilbert's Hotel

A hotel with infinitely many rooms, every one of them occupied, can accommodate a new guest if everyone moves along a room. So despite being fully occupied, the hotel will always be able to give a room to a new guest.

This is an example which the mathematician David Hilbert (1862–1943) used in his lectures. Read **Galileo's Paradox** first.

Once you see that there are no more positive integers than there are squares of positive integers it should come as no great surprise that the set of all the positive integers is no more numerous than the positive integers greater than 1.

1, 2, 3, 4, 5, 6 ...

↕ ↕ ↕ ↕ ↕ ↕

2, 3, 4, 5, 6, 7 ...

Each of the infinitely many guests can move to the room with the next higher number, and room 1 is left vacant for the new guest. None of the previous guests is without a room.

See also **The Tristram Shandy, Cantor's Paradox.**

Further Reading

A. W. Moore, *The Infinite*, 2nd edn, London and New York, Routledge, 2001, chapter 1.

The Indy Paradox

You (Indy) get 500 euros if you intend to take an exam – you are not required to take that exam to get the money. You hate exams and will avoid them if possible, but you need money. You know that if you form the intention to take an exam you will get the money and have no reason to go on to take the exam. If you know you won't take the exam, however, you can scarcely form the intention to do so.

But now suppose that there are five possible exams, one each afternoon of the week, and for any exam you take before Friday you earn the chance to get more money for intending to take the next one. So there is the potential of making quite a lot of money. You can't intend to take Friday's exam, because you know that once you had got the money you would have nothing to gain from subjecting yourself to the hateful experience. But, knowing you won't intend to take Friday's, you will see no point in taking Thursday's, so you can't intend to take that one either. You continue the backwards induction to eliminate each of the possible intentions right back to Monday's.

Yet with the chance of making the money, surely you would go ahead and fulfil intentions to take at least some of the exams.

This puzzle, due to Roy Sorensen, has a similar structure to **The Unexpected Examination**, but it is about intention rather than justified belief. It is developed from **The Toxin Paradox**. (Sorensen does not explain his choice of the name 'Indy'.)

Here is one way you might proceed quite rationally. You realize you can make some money and that you can continue to do so. So you go ahead on Monday, but postpone the decision when to stop. You know you will stop on Friday morning, since you cannot rationally form the intention to take the last exam, and that you may well give up before then if you cannot stop yourself rehearsing the backward induction. But on the preceding days there was a reason for taking an exam, namely that you could continue the sequence and continue to make money. As Friday approaches, you will have made some money, and, if you make the decision to stop one morning after you have just been given the money, when you can no longer refrain from making the backward induction, you will avoid taking an unnecessary exam.

See **The Toxin Paradox** for Gauthier's resolution, in which you adopt a policy which enables you to form intentions to take all the exams, do so, and maximize your financial return.

The problem about intention here is no mere academic puzzle, since it also arises in the dramatic real-world scenario of **The Paradox of Deterrence**.

See also **The Unexpected Examination.**

Further Reading

Roy Sorensen, *Blindspots*, Oxford, Clarendon Press, 1988, chapter 7.

The Paradox of Inference

Given the inference

> **(A)** Things that are equal to the same are equal to each other
>
> **(B)** The two sides of this triangle are equal to the same
>
> So **(Z)** The two sides of this triangle are equal to each other

we are not obliged to accept Z on the basis of A and B unless we first grant that **(C)** if A and B are true Z must be true. But then we are not obliged to accept Z on the basis of A, B, and C until we first grant that **(D)** if A and B and C are true, Z must be true. And so on ad infinitum.

But then we never get to the point when we are obliged to accept the conclusion of a valid inference whose premisses we accept.

A deductive inference is valid just when the conclusion follows logically from its premises; and the conclusion follows just when there is no possible situation in which the premises are true but the conclusion is not. So, on the face of it, accepting A and B logically commits me to Z. Why, then, must I accept Z if I accept A and B? Lewis Carroll argued that, even though I accept A and B, I am not obliged to accept Z without first granting

> (C) If A and B are true then Z must be true.

But what obliges me then to accept Z? I am not obliged to do so until I have granted

> (D) If A, B and C are true then Z must be true.

But then I am not obliged to grant Z until I have granted

(E)   If A and B and C and D are true then Z must be true.

And so on ad infinitum. But this means we are never going to be obliged to accept the validity of any inference.

Adding 'If P and Q are true then R must be true' as a premiss to an inference of the form

P, Q; therefore R

always gives you a valid inference: P, Q, (necessarily) if P and Q then R; therefore R. But that does not mean the original inference was valid. Take the invalid argument

All voters are taxpayers
Lord Macdonald is a taxpayer
Therefore, Lord Macdonald is a voter.

We certainly form a valid inference if we add the further premiss 'If all voters are taxpayers and Lord Macdonald is a taxpayer then Lord Macdonald must be a voter'. But that doesn't show the original inference was valid – in this case the original inference is plainly invalid. It would only do so if the added premiss were true, and that would only be the case if it were redundant because R already followed from P and Q.

Conclusions follow from premises in virtue of rules of inference, transformations which take us from sentence(s) to sentence; without such rules we cannot advance from the premisses to a conclusion. Piling up premisses takes us nowhere. If the inference is a simple one, as in this case, C itself encapsulates a rule of inference that licences the move from premises to conclusion. In deriving a conclusion from premises you apply rules of inference, even if only tacitly. Even if you explicitly appeal to a conditional like C to justify your inference, you do not need to add it as an extra premiss in order to make use of it, and, as we have seen, doing so provides no justification.

The Paradox of Inference

To suppose that logically valid arguments need the addition of conditionals like C to their premisses before one who accepts the original premisses is logically obliged to accept the conclusion is to treat all logically valid arguments as if they were enthymemes, incomplete arguments with suppressed premisses, like 'Socrates is a man; so Socrates is mortal'. By adding the assumed premiss 'All men are mortal' you turn it into a complete valid argument, and anyone who accepts that Socrates is a man is obliged to accept that he is mortal, given acceptance of the added premiss. Of course it is not usually necessary to do this, because premisses are normally suppressed only when they are taken for granted as known truths. Nevertheless, it is a proper response to someone who accepts the premisses of an enthymeme but not its conclusion. But, once we have the completed logically valid inference, there is nothing to be gained by adding as a further premiss, 'If Socrates is a man and all men are mortal then Socrates must be mortal'.

The paradox appeared in a little article by Lewis Carroll (C. L. Dodgson) called 'What the tortoise said to Achilles' in *Mind*, 1895.

Further Reading

C. L. Dodgson, *Lewis Carroll's Symbolic Logic*, ed. W. W. Bartley III, New York, Clarkson Potter, 1977, reprints the article referred to above. Carroll's letter to the editor, reproduced in facsimile in the volume (pp. 471–74), throws some light on it.

Timothy Smiley, 'A tale of two tortoises', *Mind*, 1995, vol. 104.

Barry Stroud, 'Inference, belief, and understanding', *Mind*, 1979, vol. 88.

J. F. Thomson, 'What Achilles should have said to the tortoise', *Ratio*, 1960, vol. 3.

For a different approach see David Miller, *Out of Error: Further Essays on Critical Rationalism*, Aldershot, Ashgate, 2006, chapter 3.

The Paradox of Interesting Numbers

17 is an interesting number because it is the only prime which is the sum of four consecutive primes: 17=2+3+5+7. It seems unlikely, however, that every natural number is interesting.

But every natural number must be interesting, for if this were not so there would be a first uninteresting number. And being the first uninteresting number would make it interesting.

When the distinguished number theorist G.H. Hardy was visiting the dying Ramanujan, he told him that his taxi had the apparently boring number 1,729. Ramanujan replied: 'No, Hardy! No, Hardy! It is a very interesting number. It is the smallest number expressible as a sum of two cubes in two different ways.' $1,729 = 1^3 + 12^3 = 10^3 + 9^3$.

'Interesting' is a relative term. In the present context does it mean interesting to ordinary educated people, to mathematicians, to contemporary mathematicians, or to whom? We shall assume, for the purposes of the present discussion, that one of these is chosen and is kept constant. The argument can be reiterated for most comparison groups. There is no sharp division between the interesting and the uninteresting, but we shall ignore that here.

If there are any uninteresting numbers there must be a first, and that it was the first uninteresting number would make it interesting. Hence the conclusion that every number is interesting.

However, suppose there are uninteresting numbers. In order to characterize the first of these as interesting, we must first characterize it as ground-level uninteresting, uninteresting because it has no remarkable numerical property. Then it is interesting because it is the first ground-level uninteresting number: call it 2nd-level interesting.

The next uninteresting number will be the first number that is not 2nd-level interesting, and thus 3rd-level intersting. And so on. The 34th of the original ground-level uninteresting numbers will be 35th-level interesting. The 900th ground-level uninteresting number, if there is one, will be 901st-level interesting. None of these seems very interesting. Indeed, being the first nth level uninteresting number doesn't seem to be an interesting property for any n greater than 1.

And if that is so, we are not forced to the conclusion that every number is interesting. The only interesting numbers will be those that have notable numerical properties (the ground-level interesting) and the first of those that doesn't – if it exists, as it probably does. The first number that Le Lionnais can find with no remarkable numerical property is 39. Thus, if he's right, we can include 39 among the interesting numbers along with all the ground-level ones. Any others will be uninteresting.

Further reading

G. H. Hardy, *A Mathematician's Apology*, Cambridge, Cambridge University Press, 1969. See the foreword by C. P. Snow added in this edition.

François Le Lionnais, *Les Nombres Remarquables*, Paris, Herman, 1983.

Roy Sorensen, *A Brief History of the Paradox*, Oxford, Oxford University Press, 2003, pp. 362–63.

The Paradox of Jurisdiction

Denise shoots Paul in February 2001 in Texas. The wounded Paul goes home to New Hampshire, where he dies of his wounds six months later, in August. Paul is not killed in February in Texas since he is not dead by then. Nor is he killed in August in New Hampshire. There doesn't seem to be any other time or place to locate the killing.

But mustn't he have been killed somewhere and at some time?

Paul was not killed in February in Texas; otherwise he would have been killed six months before he died. But wasn't the shooting a killing because it caused the death six months later? No, in February he was fatally wounded, but not yet dead. The shooting only became a killing six months later. Similarly he was not killed in Texas, since he did not die there. If you're not dead you haven't (yet) been killed, though you may have been fatally injured.

But neither was he killed in August, when the shooting became a killing, for Denise had done nothing further to cause his death since February. And if Paul was not killed in August, he was not killed in New Hampshire. Denise was never anywhere near New Hampshire anyway.

But mustn't Paul have been killed somewhere and at some time? And if not in Texas or New Hampshire, it doesn't seem he could have been killed anywhere. And if he was killed neither in February nor in August, then it doesn't seem there was any time at which he was killed either.

But we can certainly say he was killed in 2001 in the US. Perhaps to go on to ask 'But when exactly in 2001, and where exactly in the US?' is in the circumstances to ask a bogus question. The facts are simply that Denise fired in February and as a result the wounded Paul died six months later in another state. There is no further fact about precisely when he was killed, and so it is a mistake to look for one.

This type of case is significant for law – hence the name given here to the paradox. If Denise murdered Paul, then under what legal jurisdiction is she liable? The answer can make a difference to the precise law to be applied and her penal liability. For example, Texas has the death penalty but New Hampshire doesn't. So courts have to decide where and when liability is incurred.

The courts vary in the answers they give in different cases. In an English criminal case in 1971 the court had to decide when and where liability for demanding money with menaces was incurred, at the posting of the letter or at its receipt. It settled on the time and place of the posting. On the other hand, in a 1952 case the court held that the defendant was liable for a libellous broadcast where it was heard rather than where it was transmitted. And in an English libel case in the early nineteenth century the court decided that liability for a criminal libel arose both where it was written and where it was published. (These examples are given by Alan White at the end of the paper cited below, where full references for the cases will be found.) If the quietist proposal above is right, then, although the judges are required to determine how the law is to be applied, they should not do so by asking precisely when and where the demand for money really took place, as if this were a further fact they needed to discover. The facts are already fully known. What they have to decide is when and where liability is incurred.

Further Reading

Donald Davidson, *Essays on Actions and Events*, 2nd edn, Oxford, Clarendon Press, 2001.

Ruth Weintraub, 'The time of a killing', *Analysis*, 2003, vol. 63.

Alan R. White, 'Shooting, killing and fatally wounding', *Proceedings of the Aristotelian Society*, 1979–80, vol. 80.

The Paradox of Knowability

There are truths that no one will ever know, even though they are knowable in principle. If *p* is such a truth, it will be impossible to know that *p* is a truth that will never be known, for otherwise it would be possible that *p* should be both known and not known.

This is a paradox only for those – so-called verificationists or anti-realists – who believe that any truth is knowable in principle. Such a view is supported by the consideration that the meanings of our words are determined by the way we use them, so that we must be able to recognize when they are correctly applied, and in particular must have the capacity to recognize when our statements are true.

Of course many truths are inaccessible to us for physical or practical reasons. We will probably never know the exact number of human births during the present century, for example, but this is not something that is unknowable in principle. Suppose *p* is the relevant truth as to the exact number of twenty-first-century births in the world, and that no one will ever know the exact number. Then it is impossible for anyone to know that *p is a truth that will never be known.* For in order to know what is expressed by the italicized phrase you would have both to know and not to know *p*. But then the italicized phrase expresses a truth that cannot be known, contrary to the thesis that any truth is knowable.

Perhaps the essence of the knowability thesis can be retained by restricting it to exclude contradictory cases. You could never know that *p* was a truth that would never be known, but this does not mean that *p* itself is unknowable.

The paradox is due to the logician Frederick Fitch (1963), but was actually discovered by Alonzo Church.

Further Reading

*Michael Dummett, 'Victor's error', *Analysis*, 2001, vol. 61.

Roy Sorensen, *Blindspots*, Oxford, Clarendon Press, 1988, pp. 121–30.

*Neil Tennant, 'Victor vanquished', *Analysis*, 2002, vol. 62.

The Knower

(K) I know this assertion, *K*, is false.

If *K* is true it is false, because I know it; so it's false. But since I know *that*, I know it's false, which means it is true. So it is both true and false.

I cannot know that Jane is not married unless it is true that she is not married. And I cannot but know that, if I know Jane is not married, then she is not married. Anyone who understands what knowing is knows that what is known is true.

We show that *K* cannot express a statement, true or false. Suppose that it does. Then I know *K* can't be true, because if it were then I would know a falsehood. So, if *K* had a truth-value, and I knew that it did, I would know that *K* was false, i.e. that not-*K*. But I know that not-*K* is what *K* says, and so it would be true as well. But a statement can't be both true and false (unless dialetheism is correct – see **The Liar** for an explanation of this term). So *K* does not express any statement, true or false, and fails to say anything.

Notice that, in order to know whether *K* is true or not, I need to know whether *K* is true or not. Its truth value is ungrounded, as in the case of various liar sentences.

The paradox of the Knower was distilled from **The Unexpected Examination** and given its name by Montague and Kaplan in 1960.

A closely related paradoxical sentence is

(B)   I believe that not-*B*.

In fact, on the view of most, though certainly not all, philosophers who write about knowledge, *B* is entailed by *K*, since they hold that what is known is believed.

B is simply a special case of **Moore's Paradox** ('*p* but I don't believe it', etc.), and can be handled as such. On the Wittgensteinian construal of Moore's paradox, for example, to say *B* would equally be to say *not-B*. On the alternative view canvassed in the entry on Moore's paradox, you couldn't think *B* sincerely without the thought undermining itself, and you couldn't expect to communicate anything by the assertion of *B* since at the same time you would imply that you were insincere.

See also **The Liar, The Paradox of Omniscience.**

Further Reading

Tyler Burge, 'Buridan and epistemic paradox', *Philosophical Studies*, 1978, vol. 34. As Burge notes, Buridan's thirteenth sophism has some similarity to the belief paradox (Jean Buridan, *Sophismata*, fourteenth century (undated), translation in *John Buridan on Self-Reference*, ed. and trans. G. E. Hughes, Cambridge, Cambridge University Press, 1982). In this version *B* is a proposition written on a wall which Socrates reads and doubts: 'Socrates knows that he doubts the proposition written on the wall'. Replace 'doubts' by 'doesn't believe', and you have the belief paradox.

Tyler Burge, 'Epistemic paradox', *Journal of Philosophy*, 1984, vol. 81, for an alternative approach.

Richard Montague and David Kaplan, 'A paradox regained', *Notre Dame Journal of Formal Logic*, 1960, vol. 1. Reprinted in *Formal Philosophy*, ed. Richmond Thomason, New Haven, Yale University Press, 1974.

R. M. Sainsbury, *Paradoxes*, 3rd edn, Cambridge, Cambridge University Press, 2009, pp. 115–20.

Roy Sorensen, 'Epistemic paradoxes', *The Stanford Encyclopedia of Philosophy* (Spring 2012 edition), ed. Edward N. Zalta, http://plato.stanford.edu/archives/spr2012/entries/epistemic-paradoxes/.

The Lawyer (Euathlus)

Protagoras agreed to teach Euathlus law for a fee which was payable when the pupil won his first case. After the course Euathlus did not take part in any lawsuits, and the impatient Protagoras sued for his fee. He reasoned that, if he won, Euathlus would be obliged by the court to pay his fee; if he lost, Euathlus would have won a case and so be contractually bound to pay. Euathlus reasoned that if Protagoras won he would not be bound to pay, for he did not have to pay until he won a case; if Protagoras lost, the court would have decided he need not pay. Who is right?

The court should not find for Protagoras. If they did find for Protagoras they would perpetrate an injustice, since Euathlus has yet to win a case (and would still be in that position after that decision). Of course, if they find in favour of Euathlus, as they should, Euathlus is now contractually bound to pay, since he has just won a case, and, if he doesn't pay up, Protagoras can then bring another suit against him, a suit which must surely succeed. On this point Protagoras was right. This was the solution urged by G. W. Leibniz (1646–1716) – to a close variant – in his doctoral dissertation. He concluded the example was not worthy of being counted among the paradoxes, presumably since the question was too easy to answer.

Alternatively, the court may reason that if it decides to find for Euathlus he will win and be contractually bound to pay the fee, and so they should decide for Protagoras, but then he won't be contractually bound to pay and so they should decide for the pupil, and so on ad infinitum. In such an unstable state they should refrain from making any decision. (Their position would be like that of the pupils in the original **Unexpected Examination** case.) If the law allowed them to find for neither party, then Euathlus has still to win a case and is not contractually bound. In modern Anglo-American law the court would have to find for the defendant, given that it cannot find that the claimant has established his case on the balance of probabilities.

The paradox was first reported by Aulus Gellius (c. 150), and repeated by Diogenes Laertius (c. 200–50).

It has been said that the paradox has the same structure as **The Bridge,** but the latter is much simpler and cannot be treated in the same way.

No one knows whether the Euathlus case was anything but fictional. But, the pattern of argument and mirroring counter-argument has actually arisen in a legal case in modern times: the Euathlus story was cited in an American case of 1946 (*State v. Jones*, 80 Ohio App. 269), in which the defendant was charged with performing illegal abortions. For one of the abortions the only evidence was that of the woman on whom it was allegedly performed. Under Ohio law of the time, if Jones had given her an abortion she would have been a criminal accomplice, and the unsupported testimony of accomplices was insufficient for a conviction. The prosecution could, it seemed, argue that Jones must be guilty of this abortion, since, if he were not, the woman would not be an accomplice and her evidence would therefore be enough to convict him. But the defendant could argue that he couldn't be proved guilty, because, if he were, the woman would have been an accomplice and her evidence would not suffice to convict him.

On the face of it the defendant would be right: he is either unprovably guilty or he is innocent – any finding of guilt must undermine the basis for the conviction. Nevertheless, Jones was found guilty of performing the abortion in question. In such cases it was generally held that, because of the presumption of innocence – you are innocent until proved guilty – the witness was presumed not to be an accomplice. This led to the remarkable situation that the testimony was admissible and could lead to a conviction, notwithstanding the fact that the conviction undermined the probative value of the testimony.

Further Reading

Peter Suber, *The Paradox of Self-Amendment*, Section 20, B, at http://www.earlham.edu/~peters/writing/psa/sec20.htm for the Ohio case.

The Liar
(Epimenides' Paradox)

If I say that I am lying, am I telling the truth? If I am, I am lying and so uttering a falsehood; but if I am not telling the truth I am lying, and so I *am* telling the truth.

So my utterance is both true and false.

Some Different Forms of the Liar

Simple Liar

The example above is the simplest form of the paradox. To say I am lying is in part to say that I am making a false statement. This gives no problem if the statement I am referring to is some other statement, as it could be ('I wasn't unfaithful. No, I have to admit it. I am lying'). But a problem arises if it is used self-referentially. The trouble is that the self-referential use gives rise to the contradiction that my statement is both true and false, since if it is true it is false and if it is false it is true.

Strengthened Liar

'This statement is not true'. Here the self-referential use gives rise to the contradiction that the statement is both true and not true. There is no need to assume the principle of bivalence, that every statement is true or false, in order to derive the contradiction, whereas we do seem to need to assume bivalence to derive a contradiction from the simple liar.

The Truth-Teller

'This statement is true', taken self-referentially. Although no contradiction arises in this case, the statement is like an idle cog. If true it is true, if false it is false, but there is nothing that could make it either true or false.

A Liar Cycle

Socrates: (*S*) 'What Plato is saying is false.'
Plato: (*P*) 'What Socrates is saying is true.'

If Socrates is referring to Plato's utterance *P*, and Plato to Socrates' utterance *S*, then *S* is true if and only if it is false. And so is *P*. Taken in this way, although neither utterance refers directly to itself, both are indirectly self-referential: each refers to itself implicitly via the other. This is Buridan's ninth sophism. (For reference see Further Reading for **The Bridge**.)

Errors

(*S*) This sentence, *S*, has two things wrong it with. [*sic*]

S has its last two words in the wrong order. If there is nothing else wrong with *S*, *S* is false, in which case it does have something else wrong with it, its falsity. But then if it is false, it does have exactly two things wrong with it, and so must be true.

See also **Curry's Paradox**.

Some Proposed Solutions

Many approaches have been developed, some in great formal detail. Just three will be mentioned here.

(1) There is a simple and striking way out, developed recently and christened 'dialetheism', which is capable of embracing a whole range of paradoxes which issue in contradictions. These

paradoxes are dissolved by allowing contradictions to be both true *and* false, and holding that it is rational to accept them. This seems more paradoxical than the cases it purports to deal with, and to do violence to our notions of truth and falsehood. Dialetheism has been defended with great ingenuity, though unsurprisingly it has yet to win over many logicians. (See Further Reading below.) In what follows we shall take it for granted that truth and falsity are mutually exclusive.

(2) One major approach derives from Tarski's definition of truth for formalized languages. Tarski did not think it could be applied to natural languages, which he thought were inherently contradictory. It is difficult, however, to accept that it is improper to talk about truth and falsity in languages like English, and others have thought Tarski's approach could be adopted for natural languages.

The central idea is of a hierarchy of levels. At the bottom level there are no sentences containing the predicate 'true' or related terms. At level 1 'true' can be applied to sentences of level 0, but not to sentences of the same level, 1. At each successive level there is a distinct truth predicate which can be applied only to sentences at a lower level. 'Paris is the capital of France' is $true_1$, '"Paris is the capital of France" is $true_1$' is $true_2$ (and $true_3$) and so on. Thus no sentence can be used to refer to itself, cycles like the Plato/Socrates example above are impossible, and in **Yablo's Paradox** the derivation of a contradiction fails to go through.

On this approach, far from being univocal, our predicates 'true' and 'false' are taken to be indefinitely many distinct predicates. A further problem arises from predicating truth of sentences themselves without taking account of contingent features of their context of use. 'This sentence is true' is paradoxical only if the reference of 'this sentence' is the sentence itself; if it is used to refer to some other sentence, say 'Paris is the capital of France', as it could be, it can express a true or false statement without paradox.

Even if modifications of the position could circumvent this, there are other objections. The hierarchy has no place for a sentence like 'Every statement is true or false', which would be an improper attempt to say what can only be said with infinitely many different sentences, one for each level. A sentence like 'Everything Moore said was true' must implicitly use a truth predicate one level higher than the highest level of truth predicate Moore himself implicitly used, though we have no idea what that level might be.

For a brief account of an alternative, hierarchical approach due to Saul Kripke, which seeks to avoid these objections, see Haack, cited below.

(3) We have seen that there are cases where the same sentence is used on one occasion to make an unproblematically true or false statement, but on another its use is liar-paradoxical. This suggests a need to distinguish these different occasions of use by talking of *token* sentences. For a simple example, consider:

(L1)   L1 expresses a false statement.

(L2)   L1 expresses a false statement.

L1 and L2 are two different tokens of the same (type-)sentence, but whereas L1 is used self-referentially L2 is not. We have good reason to deny that L1 succeeds in making any statement at all, true *or* false, since there is nothing which could make it true, nothing to make it false. But L2 is not a self-referential token and can safely be said itself to express the false statement that the other token makes a false statement. Similarly

(L3)   L2 expresses a false statement

expresses a truth. But what about the 'Strengthened' Liar? Take

(L4)   L4 does not express a true statement.

If we deny that L4 expresses any statement true or false, isn't what it says true? If so, paradox has returned. But since L4 is viciously self-referential, it too fails to express any statement. You

121

can't say you are talking nonsense by talking nonsense, since to talk nonsense is not to say anything. But having talked nonsense, you *can* go on to say that it *was* nonsense, and now you are talking sense. So

(L5)   L4 does not express a true statement

expresses a truth.

The truth-teller and Curry sentences, taken self-referentially, will also be indicted as failing to express genuine statements.

This approach has the simplicity of dialetheism but does not require you to accept that there are true contradictions. It avoids the complexity of different levels of language and does not exclude sentences which ought to be admissible. It enables us to avoid paradox by indicting certain token sentences, although, if it is to be fully satisfying, we need to be able to explain *why* the sentences fail to express any statement. The key perhaps lies in their ungrounded nature: if they expressed statements, then whether they expressed true statements would depend solely on whether they expressed true statements. So you could determine their truth value only by first determining their truth value.

There are some apparently recalcitrant cases, but it is arguable that they can be handled by this approach. Consider

No use of this very sentence expresses a true statement.

If the sentence above could only be used self-referentially, it would be paradoxical, but it does have uses which are not self-referential. The reference of 'this very sentence' may be some other sentence we are discussing, and this is not precluded by using the intensifier 'very'. Consequently, if the sentence is used self-referentially, it expresses a falsehood, since it has non-referential uses which are true.

But what if a liar sentence has only a self-referential use?

Different token sentences of the same type are sentences which are made up of the same string of words. They are all *equiform* to one another. Suppose that the following token is equiform to the only sentence on the blackboard.

No sentence equiform to the sentence on the blackboard expresses a true statement.

Now, as things stand, tokens of this form, including this one, can be used to refer to other blackboards. However, we could make the phrase 'the sentence on the blackboard' uniquely identifying in our world by expanding it to include a unique identification of the blackboard's location and a time at which it bears the sentence. To avoid complicating the sentence, however, suppose that we live in a world in which blackboards have become such obsolete items that there is only one left in the world, preserved in a museum. Label the token on it B. It can be shown that all sentences equiform to B yield contradictions and need to be dismissed as failing to express statements.

However, this does not mean that we cannot *say* that the equiform sentences do not express truths, that we must accept the situation as undescribable. Far from it. After all, have we not just described it? For example, a token of the form 'No sentence equiform to the sentence on the blackboard expresses a statement' will express a true statement, since the omission of the word 'true' means that it is not itself equiform to B. We can also say, without paradox, 'The sentence on the blackboard does not express a true statement, nor do any sentences equiform to it', since that is not equiform to B. It is no good protesting that this non-equiform sentence expresses the same statement as the equiform ones, since they express no statement at all.

To illustrate the failure of the equiform tokens to express statements with an analogy, imagine that a number of people make sealed offers to buy a house and that the envelopes containing the bids are to be opened one after another. They all vainly attempt to outbid each other: each offer reads, 'I bid £10,000 more than the first offer to be unsealed'. Of course, no one has succeeded in making an offer. For the first envelope to be unsealed will contain a bid which in effect purports to bid £10,000 more than itself, which is no bid at all. The bids in the other envelopes seek to outbid that one by £10,000, but cannot outbid it unless it contains a genuine bid.

But there may be other cases which are not amenable to this treatment, and some have argued that it forces unpalatable revisions to classical logic.

Forms of the liar were discussed in ancient and medieval times. The importance accorded to the paradox in modern times is attested by the vast literature that has been produced in the wake of it during the past hundred years. It must be addressed if semantic notions like truth and implication are to be fully elucidated, just as **Russell's Paradox** had to be addressed in providing set-theoretic foundations for mathematics. Indeed, given the affinity between the liar and paradoxes like Russell's, treatments of them may be mutually illuminating.

In addition, it is related to Gödel's proof of his celebrated incompleteness theorem, which in effect showed that ('omega-') consistent formal systems of logic (systems where it is decidable whether a formula is a postulate) adequate for Peano arithmetic cannot capture all arithmetic truths. He showed how to construct a formula which expresses an arithmetic thesis but which can be interpreted as in effect saying of itself that it is not provable ('I am unprovable'). It cannot be false, for then an arithmetic falsehood would be provable in the system, which would thereby be inconsistent: so it is a truth unprovable in the system. Whereas 'This sentence is false' is paradoxical if uttered self-referentially, Gödel's formula, interpreted as the self-referential 'This sentence is not provable', avoids paradox, since it is true.

Further Reading

J. C. Beall, ed., *Revenge of the Liar*, Oxford, Oxford University Press, 2008.

Hartry Field, *Saving Truth from Paradox*, Oxford, Oxford University Press, 2008.

Haim Gaifman, 'Pointers to truth', *Journal of Philosophy*, 1992, vol. 89.

Patrick Grim, *The Incomplete Universe*, Cambridge, Mass., and London, MIT Press, 1991, chapter 1. Pages 25–28 contain a critique of dialetheism.

Susan Haack, *Philosophy of Logics*, Cambridge, Cambridge University Press, 1978, chapter 8.

Graham Priest, *In Contradiction*, 2nd edn, Oxford, Oxford University Press, 2006.

Stephen Read, *Thinking about Logic*, Oxford, Oxford University Press, 1995, chapter 6.

R. M. Sainsbury, *Paradoxes*, 3rd edn, Cambridge, Cambridge University Press, 2009, chapters 6 and 7. Chapter 7 is a good brief discussion of dialetheism (more sympathetic than Grim's).

Alan Weir, 'Token relativism and the liar', *Analysis*, 2000, vol. 60.

The Lottery

Suppose there will be only one winning ticket in a fair lottery with a million tickets. If you have just one ticket, say number 1,092, it is reasonable to believe that it won't win. But the same will be true of every other ticket, although you know that one of the tickets will win. Then, taken together, your set of beliefs will be inconsistent.

Although I believe of each ticket that it won't win, I will not accept the conjunction of all of those beliefs, nor indeed conjunctions that include most of them. I won't believe, for example, that the winning ticket will not be among the first 900,000 tickets. But even if we accept that rationality does not require us to believe all the logical consequences of our beliefs, we are still left with an inconsistent set of beliefs.

Suppose then that I believe of each ticket that it will lose, but that I believe that the conjunction of all those beliefs is false, since I believe that among the tickets one of them will be drawn as the winner. One of those beliefs must be false: given that one of the million will be the winning ticket, there is a false belief among those of the form *Ticket n will not win*. However, the other 999,999 beliefs of that form will be true. Since I also believe there will be a winning ticket, a million out of my million and one beliefs will be true, which is a high ratio: isn't the single false belief a low price to pay for all the true ones? The reasons we give elsewhere for accepting an inconsistent set of statements in the case of the simple **Preface** paradox lend support to this.

Indeed the lottery paradox and the paradox of the preface are sometimes treated as mutual variants. But there are significant differences:

The Lottery

(1) The statements in the body of a book are likely to be mutually supportive, unlike the statements about each lottery ticket.

(2) We know for certain that there is a false belief among those of the form *Ticket n will not win*. (So there is no analogue for the lottery of the strengthened preface paradox.)

(3) If people believed it was absolutely certain that any given ticket would lose, why would they buy one? It seems that when they learn the result of the draw, then they will come to know their ticket has lost – except in the unlikely event of their winning. They didn't know that before (so didn't reasonably believe it either), nor did they think they did. Perhaps they believe of each ticket only that it is virtually (though not completely) certain that it won't win.

But there are other beliefs to which we can't attach numerical probabilities and which we don't feel we need to qualify as not completely certain, though we would think the chances of their being false were at least as high as that of the belief about an individual ticket. Should it make such a difference that there would be no way of quantifying those chances? For example, Brian travelled in an aeroplane which was blown up in mid-air, and no one has reported seeing him since. We believe, reasonably enough, that he is dead – even though there is a recorded case of a fluke survival of a mid-air explosion. Equally, it is surely reasonable to believe that my keys will be in the drawer in a few seconds' time if I have just put them there. A clever trickster might extract them from the drawer immediately without my knowledge, but this is so unlikely in the circumstances as not to make my belief unreasonable – I do not have to hedge it.

If we order our beliefs in terms of their strength we might be able to get round this. We could then say that the subjective probability we should rationally attach to our belief that our ticket will lose is less than 1, though still as high as many of the beliefs we would ordinarily count as knowledge. This is compatible with attaching zero probability to the conjunction of one million conjuncts of the form *Ticket n will not win*. In consistency we would then have to treat the preface paradox in a similar way.

We pass on to two further proposals.

(a) The mid-air explosion is causally connected to my belief that Brian is dead, and my belief that the keys will still be in the drawer in a few seconds' time is causally connected to my having put them there; and in both cases I am aware of these connections. What causes my belief in each case also causes what I believe. The explosion kills Brian and putting the keys in the drawer causes them to be there during the next few seconds. But does the fact that 999,999 tickets will lose, which accounts for my belief that my ticket will lose, cause my ticket to lose? My ticket's losing cannot cause my belief, and it may seem that the loss and the belief do not have any common cause, since the statistical fact that my chance of winning is only one in a million is causally inert. So argues Nelkin, for example, in the paper cited below. But this is a mistake. The fact that the lottery is set up so that only one of the million tickets will win is a causal antecedent of the outcome.

(b) There is a currently popular account of knowledge which extends to reasonable belief, and which offers a neat way of dealing with the lottery paradox. On this view you know a proposition if it is true in every relevant alternative possibility not eliminated by your evidence. Whether a possibility is *relevant* depends on the context. For example, among the relevant possibilities are those you are, or ought to be, aware of. Now if I buy a lottery ticket, knowing that just one of the million tickets will win, my ticket's being the winner is a possibility of which I am, or at least ought to be, aware, and one I am in no position to rule out entirely. It is relevantly similar to the ticket which will win. So I don't know, and it isn't reasonable for me to believe, that I will lose, though of course it is perfectly reasonable for me to believe that it is highly probable that I will lose. But in ordinary contexts the possibility of Brian's surviving the mid-air explosion, and the possibility of the dextrous trickster immediately extracting my keys, are not relevant, and I do not need to be able to eliminate them in order for the beliefs in Brian's death and the location of the keys in the near future to be reasonable ones. However, if a sceptic raises these possibilities then they become relevant, and those beliefs cease to be reasonable.

But can knowledge and reasonable belief disappear so easily? It would be only too easy to undermine any knowledge claim or reasonable belief by raising a sceptical possibility, just by saying you could be a brain in a vat, for example, or that you could be dreaming or hallucinating.

The paradox is due to Henry E. Kyburg (1961).

Further Reading

John Hawthorne, *Knowledge and Lotteries*, Oxford, Clarendon Press, 2004.

David Lewis, 'Elusive knowledge', *Australasian Journal of Philosophy*, 1996, vol. 74. Reprinted in his *Papers in Metaphysics and Epistemology*, Cambridge, Cambridge University Press, 1999. For the relevant alternatives view.

Dana K. Nelkin, 'The lottery paradox, knowledge, and rationality', *Philosophical Review*, 2000, vol. 109.

Roy Sorensen, 'Epistemic paradoxes', *The Stanford Encyclopedia of Philosophy* (Spring 2012 edition), ed. Edward N. Zalta, http://plato.stanford.edu/archives/spr2012/entries/epistemic-paradoxes/.

Lycan's Paradox

The probability of (M) 'Most generalizations are false', given M itself, and the fact that it is a generalization, is less than a half. But the probability of any contingent statement given itself is 1. So 1 is less than a half.

The idea behind this paradox depends on the claim that the probability of a generalization, given that most generalizations are false, is less than a half. It doesn't matter whether M is true or not: the question is what the probability of a generalization is *on condition that* it is true. The paradox is framed in terms of contingent statements since necessary statements have the probability 1, because they have to be true.

If we take the generalization 'All machines in motion dissipate energy', we have good reason to assign a higher probability than a half to it. Even given that most generalizations are false, we have good reason to think that this is one of the minority which are true. But the paradox is stated in such a way that any outside knowledge is precluded from the assessment. We are to give the probability of M simply given M. However, M is not simply a generalization, it is the generalization that most generalizations are false. So, given that it is true, *it* must be among the true minority. We therefore have no reason for assigning a probability of less than a half, and the paradox is dissolved.

William G. Lycan presents the paradox in his short paper 'Most generalizations are false', in *Pacific Philosophical Quarterly*, 1984, vol. 65.

The Paradox of the Many

> Tibbles the cat is sitting on the mat. Tibbles minus any one of 1,000 hairs is also a cat. If any one of those hairs had been missing we should still have had a cat there on the mat. So it seems we have 1,001 different cats on the mat, for Tibbles has precisely the hairs he does at the time, and so cannot be identical with any of the cats with only 999 hairs.

His hairs are part of what composes Tibbles. But if we say that Tibbles is made up, in part, of 1,000 hairs, it seems we also have to admit that there are 1,000 other cats, each made up in part of 999 of the hairs but without one of them. So we have a superfluity of cats.

At the time, however, only one of these is Tibbles, since Tibbles still has all 1,000 of the hairs intact. And all we need to do is to recognize that the other 999 are merely parts of Tibbles, parts of a cat. The fact that Tibbles doesn't lose his identity if he loses one of the hairs doesn't mean that the 1,000 hairs are not part of him now. There is only one cat on the mat. Tibbles minus one of the hairs *would* constitute a cat if that hair had already fallen out, but it hasn't. And it may fall out in future, in which case the constitution of Tibbles would have changed a little. But then the constitution of animals and people is constantly changing.

Suppose, however, that Tibbles has moulted and there is a hair hanging loosely off him. It is indeterminate whether the hair is part of Tibbles. If Tibbles is to be counted as a vague object because he has an indeterminate boundary, then we still have just one cat. But many philosophers regard vagueness as wholly linguistic: the world is completely determinate and vagueness, they claim, is solely a feature of our language. Then we may have a number of distinct but overlapping collections of molecules, none of which is determinately named by 'Tibbles'. In that case we are still not forced to conclude that *Tibbles* is many. True we have many distinct overlapping collections of molecules, but we need not admit that there are many cats on the mat. Suppose for simplicity that there are only two cat-like collections of molecules on the mat, which differ only in that one includes the hanging hair. It is indeterminate which of these is Tibbles, but you could not properly say *that* if there were two Tibbles on the mat.

The puzzle about Tibbles is related to the ancient problem posed by the stoic philosopher Chrysippus (*c.* 280–*c.* 207 BC). Theon consists of Dion, except for Dion's left foot. If Dion's left foot is amputated, how many men do we have? Two? Dion can survive the amputation and Theon has been unaffected. Has Theon been turned from part of a man into a whole man, identical but distinct from Dion? We can avoid positing two men at the same place by recognizing that 'Theon' was never the name of a man, but of a physical part of a man, which, together with the left foot, made up the body of Dion. After the amputation Dion's body is made up entirely of the part that was dubbed 'Theon'.

For more puzzles about identity *see* **Heraclitus' Paradox** and **The Ship of Theseus.**

Further Reading

Michael B. Burke, 'Dion, Theon, and the many-thinkers problem', *Analysis*, 2004, vol. 64.

David Lewis, 'Many, but almost one', in J. Bacon, K. Campbell and L. Reinhardt, eds, *Ontology, Causality and Mind*, Cambridge, Cambridge University Press, 1993.

E. J. Lowe, 'The problem of the many and the vagueness of constitution', *Analysis*, 1995, vol. 55.

Peter Unger, 'The problem of the many', *Midwest Studies in Philosophy*, 1980, vol. 5.

The Monty Hall Paradox

There are three doors, with a prize behind just one of them.
The contestant picks a door but does not open it yet. She knows
that the game host, Monty Hall, knows where the prize is and,
when he opens another door to reveal nothing behind it, that
he has used his knowledge to do so. The host then offers the
opportunity of changing doors. She will double her chances of
winning by accepting this offer.

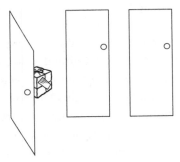

This paradox simply illustrates popular confusion about probability, and perhaps would not be worth including if it were not
for the fact that even some academic mathematicians, among them
the great number theorist Paul Erdős, at first vehemently refused
to accept that swapping was advantageous. After all, either the
other unopened door conceals the prize or the one first picked does.
Doesn't that make it equally likely that either of those two doors
has the prize behind it?

It does not. When the contestant first picks a door the chance
that it has the prize is ⅓. She knows that the host will be able to
open a door concealing no prize, since at least one of the other
doors must be a loser. Hence she learns nothing new which is

relevant to the probability that she has already chosen the winning door: that remains at $\frac{1}{3}$. Since if she swaps she will not choose the door the host has just revealed to be a loser, the opportunity to swap is equivalent to the opportunity of opening both the other doors instead of the one she has picked, which clearly doubles her chances of winning.

It would be different if another contestant picked a door which turned out to be a loser. That would raise the chance that her door was the winner from $\frac{1}{3}$ to $\frac{1}{2}$. By contrast with the host, whose chance of opening a losing door was 1, since he knew where the prize was, the other contestant's chance is only $\frac{2}{3}$. She would still have opened it had it contained the prize. The unopened doors are now equally likely.

How can this be if in both cases you learn that one of the other doors is a loser? The contrast with the host's choice is this. Unless the contestant has picked the winning door originally, the host has used his knowledge to isolate the winning door for her by opening the other empty one. But the other contestant who opens a door which happens to be a loser has no knowledge of the contents of the unpicked door to guide her in her choice. So it remains as likely to be the winner as the one originally picked by the first contestant. In this case the offer of the swap is not equivalent to having been offered both the other doors before the other contestant opens a door. The other contestant may open the winning door and then it will be too late to offer a swap.

The contrast might be easier to understand if we consider an array of 100 boxes just one of which contains the prize. The first contestant picks a door and then the host uses his knowledge of where the prize is to open 98 losing doors. The contestant has a 1 per cent chance of having picked the prize door. If she hasn't, the host has isolated the prize door by leaving it closed. By accepting the offer of a swap she increases her chance of winning to 99 per cent. If, on the other hand, other contestants open 98 doors and they all turn out losers, the chance that the first contestant has the winning door keeps increasing until it is 50 per cent. They cannot be knowingly isolating the winning door for her, since they don't know where the prize is.

What finally persuaded Erdős was the use of the Monte Carlo method, a random computer simulation of repeated trials. Suppose there are two players in the simulation: Arthur who never switches and Barbara who always does. If they play 300 times, Arthur will win around 100, Barbara twice as often, around 200 times, losing only on the 100 occasions on which her original choice was right.

No doubt some of the resistance to the correct diagnosis of the Monty Hall paradox was due to failure to appreciate the difference made by the fact that the contestant knew the host was using his knowledge to open a losing door.

What if the contestant does not know whether the host knows the location of the prize (and if so whether he will make use of it)? Unless she is certain that he doesn't know or won't make use of the knowledge if he does, it still makes sense to swap, since there is some chance that he has isolated the winner for her. Swapping will not double her chance of winning but it will raise it to between $\frac{1}{2}$ and $\frac{2}{3}$, which will therefore be greater than the current probability that she has got the winning door already.

The Monty Hall dilemma became famous when it was discussed in the 'Ask Marilyn' column of the American magazine *Parade* in 1990.

Further Reading

Paul Hoffman, *The Man Who Loved Only Numbers*, London, Fourth Estate, 1998, pp. 233–40.

Moore's Paradox

> Although it may be true that Marilyn committed suicide and that I don't believe she did, I cannot intelligibly say 'Marilyn committed suicide but I don't believe it'.

Moore's paradox concerns utterances of the form 'p but I don't believe that p', as in the example above, and 'I believe that p but not-p'. Because both parts of the utterance, for example both p and 'I don't believe that p', could be true, the utterances do not seem to be self-contradictory. And although my uttering p implies that I believe it, this is not in virtue of a *logical* implication, for if p entailed that I believed that p, it would follow from my not believing p that it was not the case that p. But clearly it doesn't follow from 'I don't believe that Marilyn committed suicide' that Marilyn did not commit suicide.

Of course, if I uttered 'Marilyn committed suicide but I don't believe it' seriously, you would probably take me to mean simply that I found the suicide incredible, or that I don't believe the official story that she committed suicide. What we want to explain is the oddity of the utterance in its literal interpretation.

Wittgenstein thought that the Moorean utterances came close to self-contradiction. If I say I believed that p I am reporting a past belief, and if you say that I believe that p you are reporting my current belief. But if I say that I believe that p I am not reporting my belief so much as expressing it. And that is what I am doing if I simply say that p. Of course I may be lying, I may be insincere, but expressing my belief is what I am purporting to do. Typically, if I say 'I believe that p' rather than just p, I am evincing a certain hesitancy. But, Wittgenstein reminds us, 'Don't regard a hesitant assertion as assertion of hesitancy' (*Philosophical Investigations*,

IIx, p. 192e). So, in effect, in uttering '*p* but I don't believe it' I am saying '*p* but maybe not-*p*', which does come close to self-contradiction.

Wittgenstein was struck by the asymmetry between 'I believe that *p*' and 'You believe that *p*'. I know what you believe by listening to what you say and watching how you behave, but I do not need to observe myself before I can express my beliefs. If asked why I believe Marilyn did not kill herself, I will not normally talk about myself but about Marilyn. If I have any reasons for that belief and don't just hold it as a hunch, my reasons for *believing* that she did not kill herself will be reasons why she didn't kill herself. I will not have separate reasons for the suicide and for my belief in it.

It was Wittgenstein, in fact, who was responsible for naming this problem after Moore, regarding it as Moore's greatest insight because of what it revealed about believing. The asymmetry between first-person and second-person uses is incompatible with logical behaviourism about belief, the view that to believe that *p* is simply to behave as if *p*. For, if logical behaviourism were correct, I would be reporting a behavioural disposition in saying that I believed that *p*. Logical behaviourism is widely rejected today, and has been replaced in popularity by functionalism, which construes mental states in terms of their causal relations to sensory inputs, behavioural outputs and to each other.

Ponzo illusion

Consider a simple optical illusion, like the Ponzo illusion illustrated above. The appearance of the upper stick (A) being longer than the lower (B) does not change when we discover they are really equal in length. Suppose I continue to behave as if the upper one is longer, picking it up if I want a stick longer than the lower one, for example. On both the behaviourist and functionalist views I can say 'I believe A is longer than B, but it isn't'. But if this were the right way to describe the case, the utterance would not be self-defeating. If this is right it constitutes a criticism of behaviourism and functionalism.

There is an affinity between the utterance 'I believe that p' and what have been called 'performative utterances'. For example, the utterances 'I say that Marilyn killed herself', 'I warn you to keep away', and 'I promise to keep away' make explicit that they are respectively an assertion, a warning and a promise. To utter the first sentence *is* to say that Marilyn killed herself, to utter the second *is* to warn you to keep away, and to say that you promise to keep away *is*, in appropriate circumstances, to promise to keep away. But you can make the assertion, the warning and the promise without making the force of your utterance explicit. You can just say 'Marilyn killed herself', 'Keep away!', and 'I will keep away'. In his fourth sophism Buridan asked whether the utterance 'I say that man is a donkey' was true or false. His view was that the speaker is quite literally speaking the truth, since he *is* saying that a man is a donkey. But wouldn't it be more natural to count it as false, as an assertion (that a man is a donkey) whose assertive force is made explicit? Uttering Buridan's sentence about man is equivalent to just asserting, 'A man is a donkey', though perhaps asserting it with greater emphasis. In a similar way saying 'I believe that Marilyn killed herself' would be equivalent to saying 'Marilyn killed herself', while hedging your utterance a little.

On the other hand there are self-ascriptive uses of 'believe' that do seem to be about the speaker. Consider the exchange: 'You don't believe me, do you?' 'Yes, I do. I believe that Marilyn committed suicide', which may be concerned with my state of mind rather than with Marilyn's death. And we cannot divorce 'I believe' completely from 'I believed' and 'You believe'. For example, if today

I say that I believe that p and tomorrow deny that I believed that p, I am surely contradicting myself.

For these cases, where 'believe' is taken at its face value, we need an alternative approach. Now, it is not just that you cannot intelligibly and literally assert a Moorean sentence, you can't consciously think it either. Of course you can think the words to yourself, but what can you make of them? If you think that p but don't believe it (perhaps because you believe that not-p) then either you are guilty of self-deception or you have an unconscious belief. You won't be conscious of not really believing that p if you have deceived yourself into believing that p or if you believe that not-p unconsciously. In that case the thought that p is something you don't believe will not be consciously available to you at the time.

But this does not explain why you can't intelligibly *assert* a Moorean sentence. For it is perfectly possible to assert something which you don't think: inveterate liars do it all the time. So we need to explain the oddity of making the assertion.

When we assert p to tell someone something, we are doing it to let them know. True, p may not be the case. We may be wrong, but we still think we are letting our audience (the hearer or reader) know. Or we may be lying; but we are still purporting to let the audience know. Now the audience is not going to believe us if she doesn't think we believe what we are saying. You cannot have an intention to do something you realize you have no hope of achieving. Sometimes, however, assertions are made to let the audience know we know that p, as in a quiz. But again, we can't hope to convey this message if we deny that we believe that p. Sometimes assertions are confessions, in which the utterer admits that she has done something, ordinarily something bad. But her confession is obviously stultified if she goes on to deny that she believes she did it, since she is saying her admission is insincere.

Not all utterances are communicative in intention. Sometimes there is no audience present, as in soliloquies and inscriptions in private diaries. But these secretive activities would not be possible if we didn't use utterances in a communicative way at all. The possibility of using sentences in this private way is parasitic on the possibility of using them to communicate. And if there is no hope of using Moorean sentences literally to communicate, then they cannot be used in these private ways either.

Moore first discussed his paradox in 1942.

See also **The Placebo Paradox, The Unexpected Examination.**

Further Reading

Thomas Baldwin, *G. E. Moore*, London and New York, Routledge, 1990, chapter VII, section 5. (See also for remarks on the provenance of the paradox in Moore's writings. The paradox is discussed by A. Duncan-Jones and A. M. McIver in *Analysis*, 1938, and presented to Moore by C. H. Langford in *The Philosophy of G. E. Moore*, ed. P. A. Schilpp, Chicago and Evanston, Ill., Northwestern University Press, 1942.)

Michael Clark, 'Utterer's meaning and implications about belief', *Analysis*, 1975, vol. 35.

Ludwig Wittgenstein, *Philosophical Investigations*, 2nd edn, Oxford, Basil Blackwell, 1958, Section IIx.

Moral Luck

It is irrational to praise or blame people for what is not wholly within their control: 'ought implies can'. But since our actions stem from our characters, circumstances and causal factors beyond our control, and their outcome is often unpredictable, luck appears to play a large part in determining our character and conduct, for both of which we are morally accountable.

So we are morally responsible for what we can't properly be held morally responsible for.

The seminal discussion of this paradox appeared in the papers cited below by Bernard Williams and Thomas Nagel.

There are various ways in which our characters and actions are constrained. Whether people have admirable or vicious characters depends a lot on their genetic inheritance; some people are born with friendly and helpful temperaments, others with malicious and selfish ones. Their inclinations and social values depend heavily on their upbringing. People brought up in a criminal sub-culture are likely to see the world differently from those brought up in more auspicious surroundings, and to behave accordingly, yet they did not choose to be born into those circumstances. The situation in which people find themselves determines whether they have opportunities to behave heroically or commit great evils: many of those living in Nazi Germany had opportunities to do good or ill which would not have been available to them elsewhere. Our choices are constrained by causal factors not under our control, and the outcome of our actions is not always predictable. As Williams says, 'anything that is the product of the will is surrounded and held up and partly formed by things that are not'.

The role of moral luck is well illustrated in two examples of Nagel's. You rush back to the bathroom, realizing you have left the bath water running with the baby in it. If the baby has drowned you have done something awful, and will deserve severe moral condemnation; if the baby has not drowned, you have simply been careless and got away with it. A lorry driver fails to check his brakes, and, if shortly afterwards he runs over a child because his brakes fail, he will rightly blame himself for the death, although if the incident had not occurred he would merely be guilty of minor negligence.

Critics of Williams and Nagel claim that, although our reactions and judgements do not always discount the element of luck, this is merely a fact of human psychology, and that if we are to be wholly rational we *should* discount that element. When people are 'simply careless' we often do not know that they have been; but when a child dies through human negligence the tragedy usually gets plenty of publicity, and our moral reactions are fuelled by anger and distress. Negligence, they argue, is equally bad whether or not it has a tragic outcome, because once we have been negligent it is usually a matter of chance whether it has a terrible outcome, and it is irrational to hold someone more accountable because of chance factors.

The problem is that, if we try to discount all those elements not wholly under our control, there will be very little, if anything, left to judge.

If we recognize the role of luck in morality, the predominant Kantian conception of morality, which excludes all elements of luck, must be radically revised, and any sharp distinction between the moral and the non-moral called into question.

Further Reading

I. Kant, *Groundwork of the Metaphysics of Morals*, ed. and trans. M. Gregor, Cambridge, Cambridge University Press, [1784] 1998.

Thomas Nagel, 'Moral luck', in his *Mortal Questions*, Cambridge, Cambridge University Press, [1976] 1979.

Dana K. Nelkin, 'Moral luck', *The Stanford Encyclopedia of Philosophy* (Fall 2008 edition), ed. Edward N. Zalta, http:// plato.stanford.edu/archives/fall2008/entries/moral-luck/.

Brian Rosebury, 'Moral responsibility and "moral luck"', *Philosophical Review*, 1995, vol. 104. A critique of the views of Williams and Nagel.

Bernard Williams, 'Moral luck', in his *Moral Luck*, Cambridge, Cambridge University Press, [1976] 1981.

Bernard Williams, 'Postscript', in D. Statman, ed., *Moral Luck*, Albany, NY, State University of New York Press, 1993.

The Paradox of the Muddy Children

A father tells a group of children that at least one of them has a muddy face. 'Step forward if you have a muddy face', he says, and repeats this request at intervals until those with muddy faces step forward. If there are n muddy children, the n will step forward after the nth request.

But if the father doesn't tell them at the outset that at least one has a muddy face, this will not happen, This will not happen even if there is more than one muddy face, so that everyone can see there is at least one, and knows what the father doesn't tell them.

First scenario. The children at a party have been out to play and on returning the father, their host, says that at least one of them has a muddy face. 'Step forward if you have a muddy face.' He repeats this request at intervals until all and only those with muddy faces step forward.

They can all see all the others' faces but not their own. As perfect reasoners able to represent others' knowledge and ignorance they are a charming mixture of naive playfulness, unimpeachable honesty and logical acuity. And they all know this is true of the others.

Suppose just one has a muddy face. Then that child will know her face is muddy, since she will see that no one else's is. So she will step forward. Each of the others will see her muddy face, and not knowing whether their own face is muddy will stand fast.

Suppose two have muddy faces. Then at the first request to step forward no one will know whether their face is muddy. Some will see two muddy faces. Two of them will see one, but all they know is that at least one has a muddy face, so they themselves may

144

or may not have one. When no one has stepped forward after the first request, they all know there is more than one muddy face. The two that see just one other muddy face will conclude that their faces must be muddy too; the others will see two muddy faces and will not know about their own faces. So the two then step forward, and the others stand fast.

If just three have muddy faces, then no one will have stepped forward at the first two requests, because everyone will see at least two muddy faces. So they all know that more than two of them are muddy. The three who are will see just two others and know their own face must be muddy; the rest will stand fast.

So, if there is one muddy face, that child will step forward after the first request, if two, the two will step forward after the second, if three the three will step forward after the third. In general, we can show by induction, generalizing on the argument above, that if there are k muddy children, the k will step forward after the kth request.

Second scenario. Imagine now that there is more than one muddy child, so that they all know there is at least one. The father, however, does not tell them that at least one child has a muddy face. Then, surprisingly, no children will ever step forward, even though what they all know is the same as what the father told them in the original example.

Now suppose there are exactly two muddy faces. Then no one will step forward at the first request. Nor at the second, since the fact that no one stepped forward at the first will no longer mean that there was more than one muddy face. The argument will never get going.

Why should this be? The answer is that there is no *common* knowledge in the second scenario. For example, in the case of two muddy-faced children, Angela and Brian, neither knows whether their own face is muddy. At the second request, Angela cannot reason that Brian didn't step forward at the first because she saw that Angela's face was muddy, so she cannot reason that there are just two muddy ones when she sees only one other which is muddy. There is universal knowledge that there is one muddy face, because each knows it, but there isn't *common* knowledge. For common knowledge that p, everyone must know that everyone knows that everyone knows . . . that p. And common knowledge cannot be achieved in the second scenario. It was achieved in the first scenario because the father's statement that there was at least one muddy child was a public one that they all heard and knew they all heard.

In the first scenario the children, who are finite in number, do not need infinite common knowledge. If there are exactly k muddy children, then the common knowledge required is that everyone knows that everyone knows . . . that at least one child has a muddy face, with 'everyone knows that' iterated k times. In other words, k muddy children require common knowledge of degree k.

For a simple illustration of common knowledge, suppose we both know which road to take for Dover, but neither of us knows whether the other does. In this little case there is universal knowledge of which road, but not common knowledge. You then ask me whether that is the road for Dover and I say Yes. Now there is common knowledge: both know which road and that the other knows which road too.

The notion of common knowledge has been thought to have very wide application. Traffic lights work only because there is common knowledge that people will stop at red. It is not enough for me to know that red means stop if I am not confident that other people know this, and know that other people know this, and that they know those others know this, etc. Universal knowledge is not sufficient. Everyone could know the meaning of traffic lights, but they need to know that others know, etc. . . . Similarly, money could not function for exchange if people weren't confident that others knew its function, and that they knew that that those others knew that others knew, and so on. Why should I accept £100 in notes unless I know that others will accept the notes in payment, which they will do only if they are confident that others will accept them, and so on? It has even been argued that common knowledge is required for the use of language.

These claims are highly controversial, and accounts that do not appeal to common knowledge are defended by many. In particular, it is not clear why common belief is not enough. But common knowledge is one of the contenders. Admittedly, the logical presuppositions of common knowledge are far too strong to make it always possible. It requires, for example, that, if we don't know something, we know that we don't know it, which is plainly often false. But common knowledge may be realizable in specific situations and approximated in many more. (For example, bank notes do not become unusable as money if a few foreigners do not recognize them as money.)

The muddy children paradox is a variant of a puzzle discussed in J. E. Littlewood's book *A Mathematician's Miscellany* (Methuen, 1953). The precise notion of common knowledge goes back to David Lewis and the idea can be traced to the eighteenth-century Scottish philosopher David Hume.

Further Reading

* R. Fagin, J. Y. Halpern, Y. Moses and M. Y. Vardi, *Reasoning about Knowledge*, paperback ed., Cambridge, Mass., MIT Press, 1995, 2003. For a fuller account of the puzzle, see pp. 4–7.

David Lewis, *Convention*, Cambridge, Mass., Harvard University Press, 1969.

Murder

In Thabo Meli (South Africa, 1954) a gang hit their victim's head with an instrument. Believing him to be dead, they rolled him over a cliff to make his death appear accidental. But the victim actually survived the assault, dying from exposure at the foot of the cliff. In their defence, the gang argue that the initial assault was merely attempted murder, and that in rolling him over the cliff they did not intend to kill him, since they thought he was dead already. Are they nevertheless not guilty of murder?

You commit murder if you cause death with 'malice aforethought'. The *mens rea*, malice aforethought, doesn't actually require malice (euthanasia can be murder) nor premeditation, though both seem to apply in this case. Nowadays, the *mens rea* is intention to cause death or GBH. The *actus reus* is an act which causes death within a certain time. Now although the four accused intended to kill with their initial assault, the Privy Council considering the appeal accepted that the accused believed that the victim died from the assault. The second act, rolling him over the cliff, did lead to death, but since they thought he was already dead they can't have intended to kill him in this way. So the act which caused death was not accompanied by the *mens rea* for murder. The defence claimed that for the initial assault they were at worst guilty of attempted murder. For rolling the victim over the cliff they would presumably be guilty of attempting to mishandle a corpse.

Nevertheless, 'it appears to their Lordships', said the appeal judges, 'impossible to divide up what was really one series of acts in this way. . . . It is much too refined a ground of judgement to say that, because they were under a misapprehension at one stage . . . they are therefore to escape the penalties of the law.'

And surely they are right about this. The accused intended to kill, and what they did, assaulting their victim and rolling him over the cliff, killed him. Suppose, for example, that D shoots to kill P. He thinks he has succeeded when he has actually missed, yet he continues to fire at P out of rage. Some of these bullets hit P and kill him. It seems a matter of common sense (as it is a matter of law) that D is guilty of murder.

Newcomb's Problem

Before you are two boxes: a transparent one containing €10,000 and an opaque one which contains €1,000,000 or nothing. You have a choice between taking the opaque box alone or taking both of them. A Predictor with a highly successful record predicted whether you are going to take both boxes or just one. If he predicted that you will take just the opaque box he has put a million in it: if he predicted you will take both boxes he has left the opaque box empty. And you know this. Should you take one box or two?

Newcomb's problem is a challenge to the use of utility maximization, which is central to standard decision theory, a powerful tool employed by economists, statisticians and policy formers.

At first sight it looks as if you are being offered an easy chance of enriching yourself. The temptation is to take one box to get the million. If you follow the principle of maximizing utility, that is what you will do. For, if you take one box, won't the Predictor have anticipated your choice and put the million in that box? The expectation from the alternative, two-box choice, is a mere ten thousand.

But there is a powerful argument against this policy. The Predictor has already made his prediction and determined the contents of the box. Whatever you do now will not change that –

you cannot change the past. If you take both boxes you will get €10,000 more than if you take just the opaque box, and this is so whether it is empty or contains the million. If the opaque box is empty, one-boxers get nothing and two-boxers get €10,000. If it has money in, one-boxers get €1,000,000, two-boxers get €1,010,000. Either way, two-boxers get more. The two-box choice is said to *dominate* the one-box choice.

The predominant but by no means unanimous view among philosophers is that you should take both boxes, and follow the dominance principle. Suppose you do this. Then it is not true that you *would* have been a millionaire if you had taken only the opaque box. For you would have acquired nothing.

But the one-boxer will retort that if you had taken just one box you would be richer, since the Predictor would have predicted your choice and filled the box accordingly.

Suppose I say, 'If you had lit a match in that room you would have caused an explosion, because the room was full of gas.' You reply, 'No I wouldn't, because I am a very careful person and I would only light a match in a place that was not full of gas. If I had lit a match the room would not have been gas-filled.' But it is what I say, not what you say, that is relevant to deciding whether to light a match in a gas-filled room. Not everyone rules out the possibility of backwards causation, but, if we do so, then similarly we must regard the contents of the opaque box as already fixed; the only counterfactual sentence relevant to the choice between one and two boxes is the two-boxer's: 'If I had taken only one box I should be €10,000 worse off.'

But what if you knew that the Predictor was infallible? If you knew the Predictor was infallible, you would know there were only two possible outcomes. You would either get the million in the opaque box from your predicted choice of one box, or €10,000 from choosing both boxes. The possibilities of getting €1,010,000 and of getting nothing drop out, because these would only be realized if you falsified the prediction. If you choose the opaque box, there is no point in regretting that you didn't choose both and get €10,000 more, because in that case the Predictor wouldn't have been infallible – contrary to what you know. But then it might seem rational in this case to take just one box; and if it is rational here, why does it cease to be rational if it is just highly probable that the Predictor is right? (It is not to the point to object that we never could know that the Predictor was completely infallible. All we need to get this argument going is the claim that if the Predictor were known to be infallible, two-boxing would not be rational.)

Suppose that, nevertheless, rationality does dictate the two-box option. And suppose that the transparent box contains just one euro. Then, although I believe it is rational to take both boxes, I know there are distinguished one-boxers, including those convinced by the argument of the last paragraph, which suggests that I might have got it wrong. I can easily afford to lose a single euro on the off chance that I have got it wrong. That may seem a reasonable thing to do, but, if I haven't got it wrong after all, does it make it the more rational?

Of course, as a two-boxer I could wish I had thought it more rational to be a one-boxer, in which case the Predictor would probably have put money in the opaque box. But I can't bring that about by changing my mind and taking just one box, because the contents of the box are already determined. It might be a good idea to keep rereading advocates of one-boxing in the hope that I might come to agree with them. If the ploy were successful, then when I next faced the choice the Predictor would have anticipated my one-box decision and put money in the opaque box. If the ploy is successful I will now have a reason for one-boxing which I once thought bad but now think is good. The trouble is that even the one-boxer has more to gain from choosing both boxes, so that I now have an irrational belief.

But was it irrational to get myself into that position? No: it can be quite rational to cause yourself to act irrationally. Suppose a burglar is threatening to torture me unless I open my safe to let him steal my valuables, and I take a drug which makes me temporarily irrational. He starts to torture me, and while complaining about how much it hurts I encourage him to go on. He realizes his threats can no longer influence me and that his best recourse is to flee. In the circumstances it was perfectly rational to make myself irrational. (Compare Derek Parfit in his *Reasons and Persons*, Oxford, Clarendon Press, 1984, pp. 12–13.)

Newcomb's problem may seem to be a purely academic puzzle. After all, isn't the Predictor a fiction unlikely to exist in real life? But look at the discussion of the **Prisoner's Dilemma**, which has been seen (at least in its standard version) as a Newcomb problem. For another example, suppose a certain disease were shown to have a genetic cause, and that the same genetic component disposed people to choose a certain career. Should you avoid that career? This is a Newcomb type of problem, since the genetic makeup and chance of getting the disease are not affected by career choice, and avoiding that career will not lessen your chance of contracting the disease.

There is also an important example of the problem in contemporary economics. Economists have found that people's economic expectations are generally fulfilled, so the citizens themselves play the role of the Predictor. Economists believe that the way to decrease unemployment is to expand the money supply. However, if people expect such an expansion they will act to counter its advantages, and inflation will ensue. It emerges that the possible situations together with their payoffs are:

Money supply expanded:
   If expansion is predicted, inflation ensues (third best).
   If constancy is predicted, unemployment falls (best).
Money supply kept constant:
   If expansion is predicted, recession ensues (worst).
   If constancy is predicted, no change (second best).

Apparently there is a consensus among economists that governments should expand the money supply, on the ground that people's expectations are already formed (just as it is already determined whether there is money in the opaque box). If people expect expansion then expansion will produce inflation, which is preferred to recession; if they expect constancy, expansion will increase employment, which is preferred to no change. In other words, the economic consensus favours the analogue of two-boxing.

'One-boxers' would be those who argued that there were two choices to consider:

Keep the supply constant: then people will expect the supply to stay constant and there will be no change.

Expand the supply: then people will predict expansion and inflation will ensue.

Since no change is supposed to be preferable to inflation, they opt to keep the supply constant. But they have failed to take account of the fact that expectations have already been formed and can no longer be determined by the choice between the two options.

The paradox is named after its inventor, the physicist William Newcomb, and was first published by Robert Nozick in 1969. The economic example is reported by John Broome in 'An economic Newcomb problem', *Analysis*, 1989, vol. 49.

Further Reading

*Richmond Campbell and Lanning Sowden, *Paradoxes of Rationality and Cooperation*, Vancouver, the University of British Columbia Press, 1985. An anthology of papers which shows the complexity and range of this problem and of the related **Prisoner's Dilemma**.

R. M. Sainsbury, *Paradoxes*, 3rd edn, Cambridge, Cambridge University Press, 2009, chapter 4, section 1.

The Numbered Balls

From infinitely many numbered balls, those numbered with the labels '1' and '2' are thrown into a room at half a minute before noon and ball number 1 is thrown out. At a quarter of a minute before noon, balls 3 and 4 are thrown in and number 2 taken out. At an eighth of a minute before noon, 5 and 6 are thrown in and number 3 taken out. And so on ad infinitum.

How many balls are in the room at noon?

(1) None, since every numbered ball has been taken out. Give the number of any ball and we can calculate when before 12 it was thrown out.

(2) Infinitely many, since for every ball taken out two have been thrown in. So at each stage there is one more ball in the room.

Suppose that we have denumerably many balls, numbered by the positive integers in sequence: 1, 2, 3, . . . , n, ... As described above, at half a minute to noon, balls 1 and 2 are thrown into the room and 1 taken out. Then at a quarter of a minute to noon 3 and 4 are thrown in, and 2 removed. At each stage we move half way in time towards noon from the last stage, throw in the next two balls and remove the lowest numbered ball. So every numbered ball gets removed at some stage. But at each stage there is one more ball in the room than there was before.

Balls left in room

Stage 1, throw in 1, 2, take out 1:   2
Stage 2, throw in 3, 4, take out 2:   3, 4

Stage 3: throw in 5, 6, take out 3:   4, 5, 6
Stage 4: throw in 7, 8, take out 4:   5, 6, 7, 8
And so on.

Ball number n gets thrown out at stage n: thus each of the infinitely many balls gets thrown out at some stage. So it seems that at noon there should be no balls left in the room. On the other hand, at each stage n balls numbered $2n-1$ and $2n$ are thrown in, so there is a net increase of one ball. Since there are infinitely many stages, infinitely many balls should end up in the room.

So which is it? This is essentially the same problem as that of the supertask involved in Thomson's Lamp (see **Achilles and the Tortoise**). Although noon is approached asymptotically, each of the numbered balls which is thrown out is thrown out *before* noon, and replaced by two other balls *before* noon. The infinite series does not include noon itself, and therefore the state at the limit, noon, is not determined.

But mustn't the state immediately after the last stage of the supertask be spatio-temporally continuous with it? No, this does not make sense. For the supertask continues at a faster and faster speed and has no last stage.

Further Reading

*Robert Black, 'Solution of a small infinite puzzle', *Analysis*, 2002, vol. 62.

Ruma Falk in *Theory and Psychology*, 1994, vol. 4, who mentions the puzzle.

The Paradox of Omniscience

No one, not even a deity, could know everything.

No human being knows everything. But isn't it possible in principle that someone should know all truths, isn't it at least logically possible a deity should be omniscient?

However, for this to be possible there would surely have to be a set of all truths. Patrick Grim uses Cantor's theorem, that the power set of a set S is always larger than S, to show that there cannot be – see **Cantor's Paradox**.

Suppose there were a set T of all truths, $\{t_1, \ldots, t_i, t_{i+1}, \ldots\}$. The power set of T is the set of all its subsets; that is, all the sets, including the null set and T itself, that can be formed out of the members of T. Consider the truth t_1. It will belong to some of the subsets (e.g. the subset $\{t_1, t_2\}$) but not to others (e.g. the null set $\varnothing$, $\{t_2, t_3\}$). For each of the subsets s in the power set there will be a truth of the form t_1 *belongs to s* or t_1 *does not belong to s*. But since the power set of T is larger than T there will be more of those truths than there are truths in T. So T cannot be a set of *all* truths.

Grim also offers a direct argument for the impossibility of total knowledge, which is a version of **The Knower**.

Perhaps the notion of the totality of truths should be treated as an indefinitely extensible concept (for an explanation see **Russell's Paradox**). Then we could treat an omniscient being as one who could extend indefinitely the set of truths she knew. The initial totality of t_is is enlarged by adding each of the truths t_i *belongs/ does not belong to s*. From the power set of the enlarged totality are generated all the further truths of the latter form for each member s of the new power set, and those are added in. And so on indefinitely. Any truth will be included in the expanding totality after finitely many operations of this sort.

Further Reading

Patrick Grim, *The Incomplete Universe*, Cambridge, Mass. and London, MIT Press, 1991, pp. 91–94. (*Chapter 2 for the direct argument and discussion of possible ways out; and *chapter 4 for the Cantorian argument and discussion of possible ways out.)

See also *J. C. Beall in *Analysis*, 2000, vol. 60.

Paradox

What is a paradox?

Many paradoxes fit the pattern offered by Mark Sainsbury, for whom a paradox is 'an apparently unacceptable conclusion derived by apparently acceptable reasoning from apparently acceptable premisses' (*Paradoxes*, p. 1). For example, take **The Heap**:

A pile of 10,000 grains is a heap.
For any number n greater than 1, if a pile of n grains is a heap then so is a pile of $n - 1$ grains.
So one grain is a heap.

Here both the premisses are apparently acceptable but the conclusion that apparently follows from them seems obviously false. Etymologically the paradoxical is what is contrary to (*para*) received opinion or belief (*doxa*). On Sainsbury's construal it would be the conclusion of the argument that would be contrary to received belief.

The most likely move in resolving the heap is to reject the second premiss. The other possibilities would be (i) to deny that the conclusion really followed, or (ii) to show that the conclusion was acceptable after all. A case for (i) cannot be excluded, but (ii) seems ruled out here. A sceptic about vague terms would not even let the argument get started.

With other paradoxes, however, faulty reasoning from premisses to conclusion is more likely to be the culprit: in **The Arrow** paradox, the arrow cannot move in the place where it is, but it doesn't follow, as Zeno argued, that it cannot move. Further examples will be found in **The Barber Shop, Bertrand's Box, Gentle Murder, Heraclitus'** and the **Two-envelope** paradoxes, among others. These paradoxes are fallacies.

A genuine example of (ii), in which the conclusion is true after all, is provided by **Galileo's Paradox**: there really are, as its conclusion states, as many squares of whole numbers as there are whole numbers. Another case where a similar diagnosis is attractive is **The Paradox of Preference**, where it is arguable that intransitive preferences can be rational after all. And in the hospital example of **Simpson's Paradox** it really is safer to undergo surgery in Mercy Hospital, even though the overall survival rate is worse than at the other hospital.

But what, you might ask, counts as 'acceptable' and 'unacceptable'? (Un)acceptable to whom? Isn't Sainsbury's account too vague? No, on the contrary the vagueness in that account is an advantage, since what counts as contrary to received opinion will vary with that opinion. What once seemed paradoxical may cease to seem so. Thus, although Quine treats Gödel's first incompleteness theorem as a paradox, it is not usually counted as one nowadays, since we have got used to distinguishing truth from proof.

The so-called semantic paradoxes like **Berry's** and **The Liar**, and the set-theoretic paradoxes like **Cantor's** and **Russell's**, typically yield a contradiction. Of course you can produce an argument with a contradictory conclusion in the other cases by adding the received opinion as a premise: add 'One grain is not a heap' as a premise to the heap argument above, and it follows that one grain both is and is not a heap. But nothing is gained by this move. In the case of the semantic and set-theoretic paradoxes it would seem as though the conclusion, being self-contradictory, is totally unacceptable and beyond redemption: something is probably wrong with the premises or other underlying assumption. But even this is challenged by dialetheists (see **The Liar**).

Not all paradoxes naturally exemplify the Sainsbury pattern, however. In some paradoxes we are faced with a dilemma. Which of the two ships, for example, is identical with Theseus' original ship – the ship with its planks replaced or the ship reconstituted from the old planks? (See **The Ship of Theseus**.) Here there is a conflict between competing criteria. Of course, you could produce an argument using one of the criteria which yielded a conclusion which involved a conflict with the other criterion. But on the Sainsbury model one of the criteria would have to be treated as apparently acceptable and the other as apparently unacceptable, in which case it would not be clear why we had a paradox.

The same objection applies to trying to fit paradoxes like **The Lawyer**, **The Two-envelope Paradox** and **The Sleeping Beauty** into the Sainsbury pattern. In **The Lawyer**, should Protagoras win his case against his pupil, Euathlus, or should the court declare for Euathlus? There are comparable arguments for either verdict. When **The Sleeping Beauty** is first woken on Monday, should her credence in Heads be ½ or ⅓? Again, there are arguments for each alternative. In **The Two-envelope Paradox** there are parallel and equally compelling arguments that you gain by swapping and that you would have gained by swapping if you had picked the other envelope first.

Sorensen has claimed that Sainsbury's definition is too broad, because it is satisfied by what he calls 'jumble arguments', of which the following is an example. He believes that any conjunction of 10,000 of the first 10,001 assertions in his book is inconsistent (see **The Preface**). Any argument that has 10,000 of the 10,001 as premisses and the negation of the remaining assertion as conclusion is a jumble argument that fits Sainsbury's definition. For he believes each premiss and thinks the conclusion is false, since he believes every assertion in his book. The conclusion follows from the premisses, since classically anything follows from jointly contradictory premisses. (See **The Paradox of Entailment**.) But such cases are easy to recognize, and Sainsbury can exclude them.

But we can't simply say there is a paradox whenever there are arguments for incompatible conclusions, or every matter of controversy would be a matter of paradox. What is distinctive about such paradoxes is the fact that the arguments for the competing conclusions mirror one another, which makes the dispute seem especially puzzling. They are instances of what is known as an *antinomy*. (Quine calls those cases in which contradictions are derived, like **The Liar**, 'antinomies', but it is not helpful to stretch the meaning of the term in that way.)

Sometimes a paradox offers more than two options. In **Bertrand's (Chord) Paradox**, for example, we are offered three equally compelling reasons for different answers to the question about the chance of a random chord being longer than the side of an inscribed equilateral triangle, ⅓, ½ and ¼, and indefinitely many contrary answers could be defended. It may be that the question is really illicit, though in this case it turns out to be incomplete, failing to specify a method of random selection. Since there are indefinitely many different methods of random selection, there will be different answers to different questions.

There is (at least) one example discussed in this book, the so-called **Paradox of Blackmail**, which is not really a paradox at all, since it rests on an *evidently* false assumption, namely that blackmail is nothing more than a request or demand plus a threat, an assumption which omits what is crucial to blackmail, that the blackmailer *backs up* the demand by the threat, which undermines any appearance of paradox.

Further Reading

*Irving M. Copi, *The Theory of Logical Types*, London, Routledge, 1971, chapter 1.

William Lycan, 'What, exactly, is a paradox?', *Analysis*, 2010, vol. 70.

Graham Priest, *In Contradiction*, 2nd edn, Oxford, Oxford University Press, 2006.

W. V. Quine, 'The ways of paradox', in his *Ways of Paradox and Other Essays*, New York, Random House, 1966, pp. 3–20.

R. M. Sainsbury, *Paradoxes*, 3rd edn, Cambridge, Cambridge University Press, 2009, Introduction (pp. 1–3).

Roy Sorensen, *Blindspots*, Oxford, Clarendon Press, 1988.

Roy Sorensen, *A Brief History of the Paradox*, Oxford, Oxford University Press, 2003.

The Parrondo Paradox

There are pairs of losing games which if played one after the other become a winning combination. Whereas you would expect the combination of two losing games in sequence always to tend to lose.

Here is a simple game where the player always calls Heads and will tend to lose:

Simple game: starting with nothing, toss a biased coin which lands tails with a probability of 0.505. Heads wins £1, Tails loses £1. Clearly a losing game.

Here is another, more complex, game, also with Heads winning £1, Tails losing £1. Again the player calls Heads every time and will also tend to lose.

Complicated game:
- if your capital is a multiple of 3, toss a coin that lands Tails with a probability of 0.905;
- otherwise toss a coin with a probability of 0.745 of landing Heads.

So we have another losing game, though the second part alone is winning. (Contrary to first appearances, in the first part of the complicated game we use the bad coin more than a third of the time.)

However, we get a game which we will tend to win by combining the losing games in a certain way.

Winning game: Start with the simple game, and after each game choose the simple or complicated game to follow randomly by tossing a fair coin. (The demonstration of the winning outcome is mathematically rather complicated, and so will not be given here.)

It is essential that the two games be linked, so that the capital at the end of one is carried over to the next.

The winning tendency from mixing the two games arises because on average the mildly bad simple game rescues you from more of the cost of the bad side of the complicated game than it costs you of the benefit of the good side.

Here is the result of a simulation:

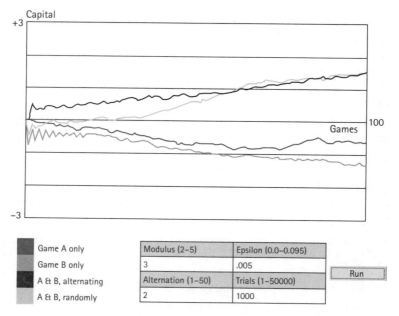

		Modulus (2–5)	Epsilon (0.0–0.095)	
	Game A only			
	Game B only	3	.005	
	A & B, alternating	Alternation (1–50)	Trials (1–50000)	Run
	A & B, randomly	2	1000	

From http://www.cs.wisc.edu/~langton/Parrondo/ (accessed 2.7.06).

The top line plots the results of 100 games with A and B alternating, the line just below it plots A and B played in random order. Both of these are clearly winning games. The lower lines plot game A only and game B only, and emerge as losing games.

The Parrondo Paradox

An apt comparison has been made with the fact that both sparrows and insects can eat all the crops. However, if there is a certain combination of sparrows and insects, a healthy crop survives, in part because the sparrows eat some of the insects.

The paradox was discovered by the Spanish physicist, Juan Parrondo, while investigating Brownian motion in thermodynamics. He devised games to illustrate the flashing Brownian ratchet. Compare how the combined game ratchets up to win: imagine you are in the middle of a long staircase, and go up one step on winning and down one on losing. The combined game should take you to the top, whereas if the first game is played repeatedly you end up at the bottom – and similarly with the second.

There are possible applications of this extraordinary result in engineering, biology, economics and population genetics. But you won't make a fortune in the casinos.

Further Reading

Derek Abbott and Greg Harmer in *Nature*, 1999, vol. 402, 23/30 Dec., p. 864.

The Pasadena Paradox

A fair coin is tossed until it lands Heads. The pay-offs are given
by an infinite sequence which alternates between positive and
negative values (rewards and penalties). Should you play?

As in the **St. Petersburg Paradox** the Pasadena game, introduced
by Nover and Hájek in 2004, also involves tossing a fair coin until
it lands Heads. Pasadena is a serious threat to decision theory,
since the expected utility, as we shall show, appears to be quite
undefined.

The pay-offs for each outcome are written on a sequence of
cards in a stack, a positive value meaning we gain that amount, a
negative value meaning we pay the amount:

Top card. If the first Heads is on toss #1, the pay-off is +$2
2nd card. If the first Heads is on toss #2, the pay-off is –$2
3rd card. If the first Heads is on toss # 3, the pay-off is +$8/3
4th card. If the first Heads is on toss #4, the pay-off is –$4

.

.

.

nth card. If the first Heads is on the nth toss, the pay-off is
$(-1)^{n-1}2^n/n$
and so on.

The expected utility is the sum of the utilities in an infinite
series obtained by taking each term to be 2n/n (i.e. 2/1, 22/2, 23/3,
24/4...) multiplied by the probability that heads falls first on the
nth toss, 1/2n, (i.e. $\frac{1}{2}$, $\frac{1}{4}$, $\frac{1}{8}$, $\frac{1}{16}$ . . .), with the signs alternating
between + and –. This gives $1-\frac{1}{2}+\frac{1}{3}-\frac{1}{4}$. . . . The series converges to
loge2 (the natural logarithm of 2), which is roughly 0.69. In this

case we expect to gain. (On convergence and limits see **Achilles and the Tortoise**, pp. 1–2.)

If the negative terms are changed to positive ones, the series $1+\frac{1}{2}+\frac{1}{3}+\frac{1}{4} \ldots$ diverges to $+\infty$, while the original series converges. It is conditionally convergent. Riemann's Rearrangement Theorem for such alternating series says that for any real number its terms can be rearranged to give a series which sums to that number.

So if the cards are dropped and picked up and stacked in a new order, the game has not changed. Suppose the cards are now stacked as follows:

Top card. If the first Heads is on toss #1, the pay-off is +$2

2nd card. If the first Heads is on toss #2, the pay-off is –$2

3rd card. If the first Heads is on the toss # 4, the pay-off is –$4

4th card. If the first Heads is on toss #6, the pay-off is –$64/6

5th card. If the first Heads is on the toss # 8, the pay-off is –$32

6th card. If the first Heads is on toss #10, the pay-off is –$1024/10

7th card. If the first Heads is on toss #3, the pay-off is +$8/3

8th card. If the first Heads is on toss #12, the pay-off is –$4096/12

.

.

.

One positive card is followed by five negatives, ad infinitum. The infinite series which sums the utilities $(1 -\frac{1}{2} -\frac{1}{4} -\frac{1}{6}-\frac{1}{8}-\frac{1}{10}+\frac{1}{3}-\frac{1}{12} \ldots)$ converges to $\log_e 2+ \frac{1}{2} \log_e 1/5$, which is roughly –0.11, a negative expected utility. In this case we expect to lose.

The Rearrangement Theorem means that any value, including $+\infty$ and $-\infty$, can be obtained by a suitable rearrangement. So the expected value of the Pasadena game is undefined. For the game is defined by the sequence of instructions, not the particular sequence of cards. To determine in standard decision theory whether we should choose an action we should need to know only the probabilities and pay-offs of that action.

Nevertheless, Pasadena is obviously worse than the St. Petersburg game. Worse too than the Altadena game, a variant of Pasadena in which each pay-off is increased by $1. As Nover and Hájek say 'decision theory goes silent where we want it to speak'. They believe that a revised decision theory with new axioms is needed.

One approach that has been offered, by Kenny Easwaran, is in terms of what he calls the weak expectation. Let Xi be the payoff from the ith playing of the Pasadena game. We consider the sum of the payoffs from n playing $Sn = X1 + \ldots + Xn$. Sn/n is the average pay-off of n plays. The weak expectation for the Pasadena game is that unique number x, if it exists, which satisfies:

$$\text{for all } \varepsilon, \text{ the limit as n tends to infinity of } P(|Sn/n - x| < \varepsilon) = 1$$

The vertical brackets are used for the absolute value, so that $|+2|$ and $|-2|$, for example, are both +2. $x = \log_e 2$ satisfies this equation and so is Easwaran's weak expectation for the Pasadena game.

Suppose a player repeats the game. What the weak expectation tells us is that the more times they play it the more likely their average pay-off will be close to $\log_e 2$. For very high numbers of plays, the average pay-off per play is almost certain to be very close to $\log_e 2$. So a player who keeps playing at a price less than this weak expectation is very likely to gain. (Alexander, Sprenger and Heesen argue against using weak expectation for a single play.)

Further Reading

*J. M. Alexander for criticism of weak expectations for single plays; J. Sprenger and R. Heesen for defence of weak expectations, *Mind*, 2011, vol. 120.

Kenny Easwaran, 'Strong and weak expectations', *Mind*, 2008, vol. 117, pp. 633–41.

Alan Hájek and Harris Nover, 'Complex expectations', *Mind*, 2008, vol. 117, pp. 643–64.

Harris Nover and Alan Hájek, 'Vexing expectations', *Mind*, 2004, vol. 113, pp. 237–49.

Pascal's Wager

If you don't already believe in God, then it is rational to acquire the belief, since if God does exist you can expect an infinity of heavenly joy, whereas atheists are punished in hell. Provided the probability of God's existence is finite and greater than 0, by however tiny an amount, the expected value is infinite, since any finite fraction of infinity is itself infinite, and so is bound to be greater than any finite good the atheist experiences.

It is true that you cannot just will to believe. Just try believing at will that London is the capital of France. Pascal himself was aware of this. He says you should bring yourself to believe by first acting as if you did: immerse yourself in Christian culture, take holy water, have masses said, mix with Christians, and so on. Eventually you will really believe.

However, there are many different possible gods, each with a finite chance of existing, however minute, who might grant those who believe in them infinite paradise. It was Diderot (1751–65) who provided the seed of this objection: 'An Imam,' he wrote, 'could reason just as well this way [i.e. like Pascal]'. Since there are indefinitely many such possible gods, indeed infinitely many, this makes the chance of a god's existing infinitesimal, and if you multiply the infinite by the infinitesimal you get a value of 1, i.e. a pretty small finite value.

Even if we ignore this objection and remain with the Christian God, He might not regard those who believed from the selfish motive of seeking infinite joy. (The point was made by William James, the novelist Henry's brother.)

Pascal's argument may not be sound (valid with true premisses), but most commentators regard it as nevertheless valid.

But it is not. This can be shown by the possibility of a mixed strategy like the delayed strategy offered by Bradley Monton (*Analysis* 72: 645). You decide to remain an unbeliever for many years, say fifty. As long as there is a positive probability that you will still be alive then, the expected utility is infinite. Yet you may well be dead by then and never have to believe in God. In this case, even if the premisses are true, the conclusion – that you can expect infinite joy – remains false. So the argument is invalid.

A more devastating objection comes from those who think the notion of the Christian God is incoherent, or at least inconsistent. Why incoherent? The Christian God is supposed to be all-good, omnipotent and omniscient. What is it that is supposed to have these properties – a being. But what is a being? Is being not too abstract for the properties to get a grip? And even if it isn't, the 'being' is supposed to be immaterial (ignoring His incarnation in Jesus), and an immaterial being cannot causally interact with the physical, so it can't create the material universe and sustain it. If the notion of the Christian God is not incoherent, it is arguably inconsistent. A perfectly good Creator of the Universe would not be omnipotent, since an omnipotent and completely beneficent deity would not create and sustain a world like ours with so much misery and suffering. If that is so, then the argument for the Wager doesn't get going in the first place, because the probability of God's existence is 0, and Pascal's argument requires it to be positive by however small a finite amount.

Further Reading

Ian Hacking, 'The logic of Pascal's Wager', *American Philosophical Quarterly*, 1973, vol. 10.

Alan Hájek, 'Pascal's Wager', *The Stanford Encyclopedia of Philosophy* (Summer 2011 edition), ed. Edward N. Zalta, http://plato.stanford.edu/archives/sum2011/entries/pascal-wager/.

The Placebo Paradox

Although it may be true that this pill will cure me, and also true that it will cure me only because I believe it will, I cannot believe that it will cure me only because I believe it will.

A placebo is effective if it makes me better simply because I believe it will. But if I realize it is a placebo, I can no longer believe that it will work because of any of its pharmaceutical properties. If my belief that I will get better makes me better, then it is the belief, not the pill, that cures me. The pill drops out of the picture. If a placebo works, it works via a false belief that it has intrinsic therapeutic properties. Realizing how it is supposed to work defeats the object of taking the placebo. So I can say, 'The pill will cure him just because he believes it will', but I cannot sincerely say, 'The pill will cure *me* just because *I* believe it will'. Though I can, of course, realize later that I have benefited from a placebo effect, and so say that the pill cured me simply because I believed it would.

There is something intrinsically odd about believing that my own belief is self-fulfilling, that it is true simply because I believe it is true. If asked why I believe I'll get better, the correct answer would have to be 'Only because I believe I'll get better'. But how could that be a proper reason?

Suppose I already believe I'll get better. Not for any specifiable reason, I'm just an optimistic sort of person. I know that optimism about the course of one's illness can help cure you; so when asked why I think I will get better I can allude to my belief that I will. I may not be able to offer any other reasons. But this does not mean that I have the belief only because I have it. I may not be able to explain why I had it in the first place, and it may not have been acquired rationally, but acquired it was, and not just because I had it. I would have had to acquire the belief before I acquired it in order for it to be true that I believed it only because I believed it.

I owe this paradox to Peter Cave.

See also **Moore's Paradox.**

Further Reading

Peter Cave, 'Too self-fulfilling', *Analysis*, 2001, vol. 61.
*Raymond Smullyan, *Forever Undecided*, Oxford, Oxford University Press, 1988, sections 15–17.

The Paradox of Plurality
(Extension)

A line segment can be divided, at least in thought, ad infinitum,
by halving it, halving the halves, and so on without end. So it
must be made up of infinitely many parts. What is the size of
these parts? If it is zero the line would have no length, if it is
some non-zero finite size, however small, the segment would
have to be infinitely long.

This is another of Zeno's paradoxes, rather less easy to handle than
the others.

Read **Galileo's Paradox** first.

Since we are considering dividing the segment not physically
but in thought, this is a paradox about the abstract geometrical
line. Each halving of a part of a finite line determines a shorter
interval, so that denumerably many halvings can determine a nest
of intervals which have only one point in common.

The number of points on a continuous line segment is non-
denumerable, that is, uncountably infinite (see note below). So
how can a continuous line segment be composed of uncountably
many points?

Because the line is finitely long, each point must have zero
length, since if there were infinitely many points of equal positive
length, however short, the whole line would be infinitely long. But
how can the line have a finite length if its constituent points each
have zero length? Intuitively the sum of many zeros must be zero,
and this is certainly true if they are finitely many, and even if they
are countably infinite. But there is no defined sum of *uncountably*
many lengths, whether they are positive or all zero: the sum of
uncountably many zeros is no more defined than is division by

zero. So it doesn't follow that the line has zero length. Indeed the length of a segment *must* be independent of the number of points in it, since there are continuum-many points in every segment – a one-millimetre line has as many points as a one-metre line (see Technical Note below). Thus even if uncountable sums were defined they could not give us the lengths.

So we can hold on to the idea that a finite line is composed of uncountably many points of zero length by recognizing that it would be a mistake to extend the definitions of finite and de-numerable sums to non-denumerable sums. It would be a mistake because to do so would prevent us from formulating a consistent theory of measure – a consistent theory of length, areas and volumes.

Nowadays this is handled mathematically by what is called 'measure theory', which deals with sets of points, 'point sets', rather than individual points. And the halvings mentioned above are really operations on point sets. An interval is a set, and when we halve an interval we halve it into two sets.

Technical Note: the Continuous Line

The real numbers (reals) in the half-open interval (0, 1], for example, are all correlated one-to-one with the distinct points on a finite continuous line. Each of these reals can be represented by a non-terminating infinite fraction. Suppose that they are expressed in binary notation – strings of ones and zeros – and that each is encoded by a set of integers such that integer i belongs to the set if and only if the ith digit in the binary expansion is 1. For example, 0.10101 ... 01 ... will be encoded as the set of odd numbers. Then the set of reals in (0, 1] is represented by the set of all infinite subsets of positive integers. This is what you get if you drop all the finite sets from the power set of the positive integers, which is said to have 'continuum-many' members – dropping the finite sets does not affect its cardinality (size).

Above, we said that denumerably many successive halvings of a line segment can determine nests of segments each with a single point in common. Suppose the segment is one unit long. Then the real number associated with a point, expressed as an infinite binary fraction, is determined by the halvings in the following way. Each time a segment is halved, if the point is in the left-hand segment the next digit of the binary fraction associated with it is a '0', if in the right-hand segment, a '1'. If the point is itself the point at which the segment was halved it is to be included in the left half. Thus each denumerable sequence of segments obtained from such a halving process associates a unique infinite binary fraction with the unique point that belongs to every member of that sequence. Likewise, it can be shown that each successive non-terminating binary fraction determines a unique nest of intervals in which each interval is a proper subset of its predecessor, so that their intersection is a unique unit point set (because the lengths tend to zero). So each of the uncountably many (non-terminating) infinite permutations of '0's and '1's after '0.' both determines and is determined by one of the sequences of nested intervals.

This again proves the non-denumerability of the line segment. However, it is worth noting that most mathematicians would regard the mathematical line and the set of real numbers not merely as isomorphic but as the very same object.

The way the paradox was initially propounded may suggest that repeated divisions yield shorter and shorter intervals until we reach an interval which is indivisible because it is made up of a single point. We can now see that this is a mistake. Each interval in one of the nests described above is made up of continuum-many points, but there is a single point, p, that belongs to them all. For any point q distinct from p there is some interval in the nest (infinitely many, in fact) that does not include q. And it should not be imagined that the halving procedure generates a list of points, since there are non-denumerably many of them and they cannot all be enumerated.

Further Reading

*Adolf Grünbaum, 'Zeno's metrical paradox of extension', chapter 3 of his *Modern Science and Zeno's Paradoxes*, London, Allen & Unwin, 1968, most of which is reprinted in Wesley C. Salmon, *Zeno's Paradoxes*, Indianapolis, Ind., Bobbs-Merrill, 1970.

Wesley C. Salmon, *Space, Time and Motion*, Enrico, California and Belmont, California, Dickenson Publishing Co., Inc., 1975, chapter 2, pp. 52–58.

The Poison Hypothetical

While Arthur is travelling in a desert, Brian slips a fatal dose of poison into his water keg. Later, Chris steals the water keg before Arthur starts drinking from it. Arthur dies of thirst. Who kills Arthur?

This famous hypothetical is due to McLaughlin (1925–26). There are four possible answers.

(1) Brian. If Arthur had drunk the poisoned water, he would certainly have caused the death. But a new intervening cause broke the chain from poisoning to death, which surely rules him out as the cause.

(2) Chris, who prevented Brian from causing Arthur's death, helped Nature to kill Arthur through thirst. Mackie (p. 46), for example, argues that the concrete event which was the traveller's death was his death from thirst, and that was caused by the theft of the keg. Although, to assuage the doubts of lawyers about identifying Chris as the killer, he distinguishes facts from events and allows that the fact that he died was not caused by the theft.

It is true that causing death normally involves shortening life, and Chris actually postpones the death. However, if someone postpones a death, does that preclude causing it? Suppose A is eating in a restaurant and B slips poison into his food. A feels ill, and leaves the restaurant for home. A few minutes later terrorists set off a bomb which kills outright all those sitting near the seat A occupied. B himself would have died immediately if he had stayed. He dies from the poison next day. His death has been postponed by B, but surely B has caused it.

(3) Neither Brian nor Chris. Not Brian, because as observed above in (1), Chris broke the causal chain from poisoning to death. Nor Chris either, since, as Hart and Honoré claim (p. 241), depriving Arthur of lethally poisoned water cannot itself amount to killing. This is surely a powerful point (though Honoré has since changed his mind about it). If they intended to kill, no doubt they are both guilty of attempted murder, but that is another matter.

(4) Both. But if Brian didn't kill Arthur, then it follows that they didn't both kill him, which rules out this fourth possibility.

The competition, it seems, is between (2), Chris and not Brian, and (3), neither of them. Given the contemporary controversy about causation with its various competing views, it is not surprising that there is disagreement here.

Further Reading

H. L. A. Hart and Tony Honoré, *Causation in the Law*, 2nd edn, Oxford, Clarendon Press, 1985, pp. 239–41.

J. L. Mackie, *The Cement of the Universe*, Oxford, Clarendon Press, 1980, pp. 44–46.

The Prediction Paradox

> If all events are governed by causal laws, then every event can
> in principle be predicted. But if that is so, it will be possible to
> falsify predictions about our own actions by opting not to do
> something that was predicted. Then they wouldn't be correct
> predictions after all.

The conclusion you might be tempted to draw from this is that
causal determinism – the view that all events are subject to casual
laws – is false. But this would be a mistaken inference. (Cf.
Buridan's Ass.)

Predicting events which are under our control would be an
extraordinarily complex matter. Perhaps no one ever will predict
such an event and falsify it. However, it is enough that it would
be possible to make such a prediction and falsify it: the mere
possibility of a contradiction is enough for the argument. A contradiction would be involved in predicting, for example, that I will
go on holiday to Venice next year and then refraining from doing
so. If I don't go to Venice then I won't have predicted correctly.
But is self-prediction of this sort even possible? Maybe predicting
a future action of mine on the basis of present conditions and
causal laws is beyond my intellectual capacity. Of course I may
predict that I will do so because I have already decided to go there,
but that is a different matter. We are talking about predicting
on the basis of current physical conditions and physical causal
laws. That sort of prediction is certainly way beyond us at the
moment, despite our increasing knowledge of the human brain.
Without any reason to think such predictions would be humanly
possible, the paradox has little bite. It may be a necessary condition
for controlling our actions that we are not capable of making
predictions we could frustrate.

Note that the very different paradox of **The Unexpected Examination** is sometimes called the 'prediction paradox'.

Further Reading

Michael Levin, *Metaphysics and the Mind–Body Problem*, Oxford, Clarendon Press, 1979, chapter 7, sections 6–7.

The Preface

Authors frequently write in their prefaces that there will inevitably be errors in the body of the book – I have done so myself in the preface to this book. If what they write is true, there will be at least one false statement in the book; otherwise the prefatorial claim is false. Either way they are committed to a falsehood, and must be guilty of inconsistency. Yet the claim in the preface seems a perfectly reasonable one to make.

So extensive is our experience of human fallibility that we have very good reason to expect that no book which makes a large number of statements will be totally free of error. The author does not, of course, know which of the statements are false, and she may have good reason to believe each of the statements in her book. In any case she is committed to each of them. So the chances are that she is already committed to at least one falsehood. If this is so, to add the statement in the preface is to add a truth, and thereby increase the number of truths she states. 'He is always right', goes the Spanish proverb, 'who suspects he is always making mistakes'. Falsehood is unlikely to be avoided by omitting the preface. So we have a case where it is perfectly rational to commit oneself to each of a set of inconsistent beliefs, even though one knows they are jointly inconsistent and so cannot all be true. What the paradox shows is that we need to give up the claim that it is always irrational to believe statements that are mutually inconsistent.

A self-referential version of this paradox gives it an affinity to **The Liar**. Suppose the preface contains the sentence 'At least one of the statements in the book is false', where it is understood that the preface itself is included in the book. If there is a false statement elsewhere in the book, this concession would, it seems, be true.

But if all the other statements are true, we have a problem. In that case, if the preface statement is false, all the book's statements, including this one, are true; but then it can only be true by being false. So if all the other statements are true, this one is true if and only if it is false – which is a contradiction. Compare Moore's negative answer when Russell asked him whether he always told the truth: if all Moore's other utterances were true his reply was true if and only if false. (Russell must have been joking when he said that he thought this was the only falsehood Moore had ever told.)

The self-referential version of the preface paradox is very similar in form to the Pauline version of the liar: Epimenides the Cretan says, 'The Cretans are always liars.' (Paul's *Epistle to Titus*, 1: 12). Actually many people are liars, but that doesn't mean they utter nothing but falsehoods. We can sharpen the example by rewriting the critical sentence as 'Cretans utter nothing but falsehoods.' It would apparently be false if some other Cretan utters a truth; if no other Cretan utters a truth, it is false if true, and true if false – a contradiction again. We can treat this in the same way as we treat liar sentences in the section on **The Liar** above (solution 3). When all other Cretan utterances are false, Epimenides' sentence does not express a true statement because it does not express a statement (true or false) at all. So one could also say that, when all the other declarative sentences in the book express truths, the prefatorial sentence does not express a truth or a falsehood.

Two problems now arise: (1) The prefatorial sentence does not refer just to the tokens in a single copy of the book but to all the sentences in all the copies, in other words to certain sentence types rather than specific tokens. But perhaps this can be circumvented by construing *statement* as applying to each of a set of corresponding tokens in the different copies of the book.

(2) The self-referential sentence of the preface cannot express a truth. Can a sentence which cannot express a truth express a falsehood? If it can, then, if we did not know whether it was true,

we should not know whether it expressed a statement. Some philosophers have subscribed to a principle of significant negation according to which any sentence which can express a truth must also be capable of expressing a falsehood if negated. In which case we would have to say that the sentences in question do not express a statement, whatever the truth or falsity of the other statements in the book (or uttered by Cretans). But perhaps these examples show that the principle of significant negation is not correct.

The paradox in its original form is due to D. C. Makinson (1965) and in its strengthened version to Arthur Prior (1971).

Compare **The Lottery**.

Further Reading

J. L. Mackie, *Truth, Probability and Paradox*, Oxford, Clarendon Press, 1971, chapter 6.

D. C. Makinson, 'The paradox of the preface', *Analysis*, 1965, vol. 26.

A. N. Prior, *Objects of Thought*, Oxford, Clarendon Press, 1971, chapter 6.

The Paradox of Preference

If offered a choice between flying a glider accompanied by an experienced pilot and driving a Grand Prix car around a racing track, you would choose to fly the glider; but, if offered a choice between driving the racing car and flying a glider solo, you would choose to drive the car. If you are rational, then, given that you prefer the accompanied glider flight to the car drive and the drive to flying solo, you should choose to fly accompanied in preference to flying solo. To choose to fly solo in preference to flying accompanied would therefore be irrational.

But it is not irrational, when offered a choice between flying accompanied and flying solo, to choose to fly solo because you do not want to appear cowardly.

So it is both irrational and not irrational to choose the solo over the accompanied flight.

This is a problem for rational decision theory (compare **Newcomb's Problem**, the **Prisoner's Dilemma**), which is important for economic theory. Rationality seems to require that our preferences be transitive; that is, if we prefer a to b and b to c, we prefer a to c. We can express this symbolically as: if Pab and Pbc, then Pac. If preference is transitive then it is like height: if a is taller than b and b is taller than c, then a is taller than c. Transitivity is built into the very meaning of 'taller than'. Despite what has been claimed, this cannot be the case with preference, though, since there is no logical contradiction involved in the example above. But does *rationality* nevertheless require that preference be transitive?

One argument used to support an affirmative answer is the 'money pump' argument. Suppose you have a ticket which entitles you to fly a glider solo. Since you prefer the car drive to the solo flight, I should be able to give you a ticket for the drive in return for your ticket and some money. After that I should be able to give you a ticket for an accompanied flight in return for your ticket to drive the car and some money. But if your preferences are not transitive, and you would choose the solo flight in preference to the accompanied one, I can give you back the ticket for the solo flight in return for your ticket for the accompanied one and some money. If I keep doing this, I get money from you indefinitely, and, even if it has cost me money to acquire the tickets for the accompanied flight and the car drive in the first place, their cost will soon be covered.

It might be more accurate to say that *if offered a choice between accompanied flight and car drive* you would choose the accompanied flight; *as between car drive and solo flight* you would choose the car drive, but *as between accompanied and solo flights* you would choose the solo flight. If the italicized restrictions are inserted, then they have to be the same restrictions if transitivity is to be preserved, and the symbolic formulation in the first paragraph above was not understood as incorporating these restrictions. We can make them explicit by means of something like: if P*aab* and P*bbc*, then P*aac*, where 'P*xxz*' stands for a three-place predicate, 'S prefers *x* when offered a choice between *x* and *y*', which is not the same as the predicate for which 'P*xy*' ('S prefers *x* to *y*') stands in the simpler formulation in the first paragraph.

But even if your preferences are restricted in the way described, it looks as if you are still vulnerable to the money pump.

Yet would a rational person really be that vulnerable? Once the subject finds that she is back with the ticket for the solo flight, but with a lighter purse, she is not likely to continue to trade. And if she has complete information from the start, and knows about her preferences and their sensitivity to the image she wants to project, then she is not going to let herself be cheated of her money if she is rational.

If this is right, then it is possible to have intransitive preferences without being irrational, and the paradox is resolved.

See also **Quinn's Paradox**.

Further Reading

P. Anand, *Foundations of Rational Choice under Risk*, Oxford, Oxford University Press, 1993, chapter 4.

Sven Ove Hansson and Till Grüne-Yanoff, 'Preferences', *The Stanford Encyclopedia of Philosophy* (Fall 2011 edition), ed. Edward N. Zalta, http://plato.stanford.edu/archives/fall2011/entries/preferences/.

Prisoner's Dilemma

We have been arrested for a serious offence and put in separate cells, and we both know that our fate will be determined in the following way:

> If one confesses while the other stays silent, the confessor goes free and the other is sentenced to ten years.

> If both confess we both get seven years.

> If both stay silent, we both get a year for a lesser offence.

Assume that we both want to minimize our sentences and that we are both rational. Then I will confess. For, if you confess then I had better do so since otherwise I get ten years, and if you stay silent I will go free if I confess. So whatever you do I am better off confessing. Since, given the assumption of rationality, you will decide in the same way, we will both confess and get seven years each. Yet we would both have been better off if we had stayed silent and only got a year each.

The dilemma is set out in the following matrix:

	You confess	You stay silent
I confess	7 years each [3rd for me]	0 for me, 10 years for you [Best for me]
I stay silent	10 years for me, 0 for you [Worst for me]	1 year each [2nd for me]

Second and third best for you are the same as for me, whereas the best outcome for me is the worst for you, and vice versa.

Since I am rational I can see that if we both stay silent the outcome will be better for both of us; and since you are rational so can you. In that case won't we both decide the same way and both opt for silence? No, because if I think you are going to stay silent I can do even better by confessing. In any case, since you can too, I have no reason to think you won't confess after all. So we'll both confess.

Under the assumptions, it is impossible to achieve the full benefits of cooperation unless both parties take a foolish risk. If that seems paradoxical, we just have to swallow it. The full benefits of cooperation require mutual agreement and mutual assurance. As things stand, even if we had come to an agreement before being separated I cannot trust you to keep it.

This may seem an artificial case, of a sort unlikely to arise much in the real world. But this is not so. For example, it has the same structure as the following very realistic sort of case. Suppose two sides make a disarmament agreement which it is only too easy for each to evade by secretly retaining their weapons:

	They break the agreement	They disarm
We break the agreement	Risk of war [3rd for us]	They are at our mercy [Best for us]
We disarm	We are at their mercy [Worst for us]	No war [2nd for us]

From the point of view of realpolitik we will both break the agreement and risk war, since whatever one side does the other is better off if it reneges on the agreement. Yet it would be better for both of us if there were no war.

In any case there are many circumstances calling for multi-party cooperation, for example, reining in the proliferation of nuclear weapons, using public transport rather than private cars, or limiting wage demands.

How can we secure the mutual agreement and assurance required to achieve cooperation? To some extent this is secured by law: our system of property, for example, is both created and supported by law, with criminal sanctions against those who steal and civil compensation for those who renege on contracts. But our legal system would not function unless its officials accepted its norms and were disposed to enforce it impartially. And without general public support law cannot be enforced without terror. The best guarantee for cooperative enterprises is to inculcate and develop moral attitudes generally, to build on the degree of innate altruism to be found in most people, and to foster social pressures to keep agreements and cooperate fairly. Law can then function as a backup. (But that is not to say that this gives a solution to Prisoner's Dilemma within its own terms of individualistic rational self-interest.)

In real life, decisions about cooperation are not always one-off matters, but recur. If there are repeated choices then what you choose each time can be expected to affect the choice of the other party. If I risk sacrificing my immediate self-interest by cooperating, then you are more likely to trust me and take the same risk next time, and these decisions will be mutually reinforcing. On the other hand, if I find you don't act cooperatively I will not do so in future, since I cannot then reap the benefits of cooperation and I lay myself open to exploitation. This 'tit for tat' pattern of responses turns out to be the most prudent course of action in what is called 'iterated Prisoner's Dilemma', a claim which has been verified empirically by computer simulations. There is reason to think that it is part of our evolutionary legacy to be disposed to reciprocate in this way – as the human inclinations to express gratitude and seek revenge testify: we are naturally inclined to repay favours and to retaliate against those who harm us.

In the case where both parties know the other will behave rationally, iterated Prisoner's Dilemma gives rise to an additional paradox. Neither party can act cooperatively in the hope of inducing cooperation from the other because a backward induction shows that the dominant choice of defection will be made every time. There will be no 'tit for tat' to be expected when the last choice is made, so it will be made selfishly. But then the same will apply to the choice before that, and so on backwards to the first choice. (For another example of this type of argument see **The Unexpected Examination**.) However, for the backward induction to get started, the parties need to be sure they will recognize the last choice when they come to it, and that is not commonly how things are in real life. Nor, indeed, in real life are we generally confident that others will always act rationally.

Prisoner's Dilemma has been regarded as a **Newcomb Problem**. Just as two-boxers will argue that I am better off if I take both boxes, whether or not the opaque box has money in it, so I am better off if I confess, whether or not the other prisoner does. In both cases one option is said to 'dominate' the other.

Prisoner's Dilemma was devised around 1950 by a social psychologist and an economist to test a theorem in game theory.

See also **Newcomb's Problem**.

Further Reading

*Richmond Campbell and Lanning Sowden, *Paradoxes of Rationality and Cooperation*, Vancouver, the University of British Columbia Press, 1985. An anthology of papers which shows the complexity and range of this problem and of the related **Newcomb's Problem**.

D. Parfit, *Reasons and Persons*, Oxford, Clarendon Press, 1984, chapters 2–4.

R. M. Sainsbury, *Paradoxes*, 3rd edn, Cambridge, Cambridge University Press, 2009, pp. 82–8.

The Prosecutor's Fallacy

Sally Clark was convicted of killing two of her babies. The prosecution expert claimed that the chance she was innocent was one in 73 million, got by squaring the chance of one baby dying without known physical cause. But the chance of her guilt was well below the threshold for proof beyond reasonable doubt. How can this be so?

It was claimed that, since the chance of one baby dying of sudden infant death syndrome (SIDS) is 1 in 8,544, the chance of two such deaths in the same family was 1 in 73 million. This was arrived at by squaring 8,544 (just as, if a fair coin is tossed twice, the chance of its landing Heads twice is $0.5 \times 0.5 = 0.25$). However, this assumes that the two deaths are independent. But once one baby has died of SIDS, the chance of a second is not 1 in 8,544 but much less, 1 in 200. So the chance of two unexplained dying in the same family would not be 1 in 73 million but 1 in $(8,544 \times 200)$, i.e. 1 in 1.7 million. This still looks very incriminating, of course.

That is before the fallacy is committed. Given that we have two unexplained baby deaths in the same family, we need to consider the competing explanations: SIDS and murder. The chance of two murders of babies in the same family is 1 in 2.2 billion. Even allowing for the additional evidence of haemorrhages in the brains and eyes which are five times more likely in murder than in SIDS, we get a chance of murder in this case of around 5 in 1299 (about 1 in 260). Rather than her chance of innocence being 1 in 73 million, as claimed in court, it was actually nearer 259 in 260 – a probability of innocence of 99.6%! (Even if the two deaths were independent and 1 in 73 million was correct, with these figures the probability of her innocence given the evidence, including blood in eyes multiplier, is 86%!) The court considered the probability of two baby deaths in one family given that the defendant was innocent instead of the probability of innocence given that a mother had two dead babies.

What in general is going wrong here is that the low probability of the evidence makes it seem as if the probability of guilt is very high. But that appearance arises from the fallacy of confusing two conditional probabilities. What we want is the probability of the hypothesis of innocence given the evidence, but what we have is the probability of the evidence given the hypothesis of innocence. This is what generates the paradox. What seems a very high probability of guilt can turn out to be a low one just because at one and the same time the probability of the evidence given innocence can be low and the probability of innocence given the evidence can be high.

A similar mistake was made in the case of the Birmingham Six (found guilty of bombing two public house and killing 21 people). Swabs from the hands of two them showed they had nitroglycerine on them, from which it was concluded that it was 99% certain they had handled explosives. The men claimed they had been playing cards and they could have caused the swab results. It was later shown that even soap could cause such results. The forensic results were accepted as discredited in the appeal in 1991, which released the Six.

Detecting the fallacy is evidently of great importance, since it has led to serious miscarriages of justice.

Further Reading

Bernard Robertson and G. A. Vignaux, *Interpreting Evidence*, Chichester, Wiley, 1995, esp. pp. 91–3.

Royal Society of Statistics on Sally Clark case: http://www.sallyclark.org.uk/RSS.html

The Paradox of the Question

Is the question, 'What is one of the most useful pairs of question and answer?', together with its answer, one of the most useful question and answer pairs? Suppose it is given as the question part of its own answer. Then it is an incorrect answer because it is so uninformative. But since all the correct answers will be highly useful, it is a highly useful question to ask after all. So it is correct to give it as part of its own answer only if it isn't correct; and, if it isn't correct to do so, it is.

There are some questions whose answers would be of great value to us if we had them. For example, *How can nuclear war be avoided? What is the solution to world poverty? How can democracy be safeguarded from erosion?* (We are to imagine that we may put our questions to an angel who is able to answer them.) Such questions might appear in correct answers to the question

(Q)   What is an example of a question and answer where the question is one of the best we could ask?

But isn't this question itself one of the best we could ask? It has correct answers like *What is the solution to world poverty?* together with a statement of the solution (assuming, as we shall for the sake of argument, that there is one). So let us ask whether the answer

(A)   That question Q and this answer A.

is a correct answer to Q. If it *is* a correct answer, its uselessness makes it an incorrect answer to Q. But if it is incorrect, all the correct answers will be so useful that this answer will be correct too. In other words, it is a correct answer if and only if it is not, a contradiction which makes the very question Q paradoxical.

It gives further support to the approach in terms of token sentences in our treatment of **The Liar** above to note that it can be used to handle this paradox too. If 'questions' in Q means 'token questions' and 'that question' in the answer refers back to the token Q, then the answer is straightforwardly false, since its answer fails to be highly informative. (In general, any token Q' equiform to Q which gets an answer whose first member is Q' will have received a false answer.) Other tokens equiform to Q may elicit more informative answers, as in the world poverty example in the previous paragraph. A more complex example would be

(Q') What is an example of a question and answer where the question is one of the best we could ask?

Answer:

Q', (Q', ('What is the solution to world poverty?', [the solution to world poverty])).

The phrase in square brackets is schematic. If we could replace it by the actual answer, it would add considerably to the value of this book.

Whether an equiform token of the type in question is one of the best questions depends on what answer it gets (if any): some are among the best questions, others are not. The derivation of a contradiction has been blocked and the paradox has disappeared.

Perhaps it will be objected that this treatment is a cheat: wasn't the paradox about question types, not tokens? Doesn't it ask for a question *type* whose tokens induce highly informative answers? But, if it is construed in this way, the answer <Q, *this answer*> is, once again, straightforwardly false, since not all tokens of Q get informative answers, as this particular answer shows. So the paradox has not reappeared.

This paradox is a recent one, introduced in the pages of the journal *Analysis* in 1997. In its original form it asked for *the best question* to ask, together with its answer. For a non-paradoxical answer to this one, see the Further Reading below.

Further Reading

*Alexander D. Scott and Michael Scott, 'The paradox of the question', *Analysis*, 1999, vol. 59.

*Achille Varzi, 'The best question', *Journal of Philosophical Logic*, 2001, vol. 30.

Quinn's Paradox

You are offered money to accept a mildly painful stimulus, and more money each time the stimulus is increased. There is a degree of pain from the stimulus so great no amount of money would induce you to accept it. But each single increment is undetectable. So there is no point at which it is rational for you to call a halt: you will always find it advantageous to accept the next degree of pain for more money, since it will be indistinguishable from the last.

Although there is a degree of agony that you would refuse to suffer no matter how much you were paid to do so, let us suppose that there is a tolerable range of pain that you would probably be prepared to accept for attractive enough payments. But it is surely irrational to stop at any point: if you were prepared to accept money for the last increment, you should be prepared to accept money for the next, since it will not increase your felt pain. But then you would never stop, and the pain would grow inordinately!

Your preferences in this case are not transitive. (See **The Paradox of Preference.**) For the money makes you prefer degree 1 to degree 0, 2 to 1 and so on, though not, say, 1,000 to 1. But the paradox is not resolved by admitting the rationality of intransitive preferences. For we still haven't found a point at which it is rational to stop.

In addition to the intensity of the pain there is its cumulative effect. For the sake of simplicity, we shall ignore the cumulative effect and regard the threshold of tolerance as a function solely of the pain's intensity. The cumulative effect could probably be eliminated by having a period of rest between each episode of pain.

Doubtless you will stop accepting the money at some point. If you go on long enough and reach a point where you wish you had stopped earlier, you will certainly stop then. But, if you do stop before that point is reached, it seems irrational to forgo extra money by refusing an increase in the stimulus which does not noticeably increase your pain.

Since it is irrational to continue to a point where the extra money you have accepted is not worth the extra pain, it may be that the *most* rational course would be to decide to stop one increment after the point where you first think that detectably greater pain is not worth the money, and resist the temptation to proceed further, even though that too seems irrational. Perhaps we have to accept that there is no fully rational solution to this problem, and that we have to live with the paradox. Alternatively, we need to revise our notion of rational choice to accommodate this sort of case, which is the moral drawn by Warren Quinn, who devised the problem.

This paradox is not simply a theoretical academic puzzle. It arises in everyday life. One more drink will not significantly affect our health, but many will; one more minute in bed will not make us significantly later for work, but many minutes will.

Compare **The Heap** and **The Indy Paradox**.

Further Reading

Warren S. Quinn, 'The puzzle of the self-torturer', *Philosophical Studies*, 1990, vol. 59.

The Racecourse
(Dichotomy, The Runner)

[Progressive form] Achilles cannot reach the end of the racecourse, since he would have to traverse infinitely many intervals. He would have to reach the half-way point, and then successively reach the half-way point of each distance remaining, traversing an infinite sequence of intervals.

[Regressive form] Before he can get to the end of the course Achilles must first cover the first half, and before he does that he must cover the first half of that, i.e. the first quarter, and before that the first eighth, and so on. He cannot get anywhere beyond the start without first having traversed infinitely many intervals.

The progressive version of the Racecourse is essentially the same as **Achilles and the Tortoise**. Indeed, it is slightly simpler, in that, instead of having to catch a moving tortoise, Achilles has only to reach the stationary end of the course; but that makes no essential difference to the paradox or its resolution. Achilles can traverse the infinitely many intervals in a finite time because each successive interval is half as long as the last. The sum of these intervals is the sum of the infinite series

$$\tfrac{1}{2} + \tfrac{1}{4} + \tfrac{1}{8} + \tfrac{1}{16} + \ldots + \tfrac{1}{2^n} + \tfrac{1}{2^{n+1}} + \ldots ,$$

which is 1. (This is briefly explained in the entry on **Achilles and the Tortoise**.)

The regressive version introduces a further paradoxical feature. Achilles seems to be prevented from even starting to run, since he cannot move beyond the start without having first traversed infinitely many intervals. And in any case there is no first interval for him to run. The sequence of intervals he needs to run is given by taking the terms in the series displayed above in the reverse order:

$$\ldots, \; {}^1/_{2^n}, \; {}^1/_{2^{n-1}}, \; \ldots, \; {}^1/_{16}, \; {}^1/_8, \; {}^1/_4, \; {}^1/_2.$$

But if Achilles can get to the end of the course in the progressive version above, he can get to any point after the start by traversing an infinite sequence of intervals. For example, he can get ${}^1/_{64}$ of the way by traversing intervals which can be represented in a series which sums to ${}^1/_{64}$. However short the distance from the start, he will have traversed infinitely many of these intervals, but they will always have a sum. It is true that in the sequence of ever-increasing intervals there is no first interval. But all this means is that we should avoid analysing his run in terms of a sequence with no first term. There are plenty of other ways of analysing it so that the question makes sense, either using finite sequences or infinite sequences with a beginning.

Further Reading

Wesley C. Salmon, *Space, Time and Motion*, Enrico, California and Belmont, California, Dickenson Publishing Co., Inc., 1975, chapter 2.

The Rakehell

It is better to feel shame about something shabby you have
done than to act shamelessly. But if you feel good about feeling
ashamed, that detracts from your feeling of shame.

A man creeps back home after an adulterous assignation, 'feeling a
tremendous rakehell, and not liking myself much for it, and feeling
rather a good chap for not liking myself much for it, and not liking
myself at all for feeling rather a good chap' (Kingsley Amis, *That
Uncertain Feeling*, London, Victor Gollancz, 1955). ('Rakehell' is
an archaic term for a debauchee or rake.) The paradox has been
extracted from Amis's novel by Richard Moran (see Further Reading
below).

If you feel appropriate shame you can reflect on it later and feel
good that you were not shameless; and someone else can approve
of your feeling. So why can't you feel good about yourself at the
time without undermining the original feeling? Because you are
now thinking of your feeling of shame rather than simply of your
disreputable act, and the discomfort you feel from your shame is
mitigated by your feeling of complacency. That is why Amis's
adulterer ends up 'not liking [himself] at all for feeling rather a
good chap', though he'd better not feel good about *that*!

The phenomenon is not peculiar to moral feelings. To the
extent that attention to the object of a feeling is necessary to it,
any introspection of that feeling is likely to weaken it. If I am
apprehensive about a forthcoming interview, then reflection on
my feelings can help to take my mind off the interview. If a woman
puzzles about why she feels so jealous of a colleague's success,
she ceases to concentrate exclusively on that success and the
jealous feeling will tend to weaken. This is why it helps to talk

about your feelings if you suffer disappointment or grief, whereas people who are overjoyed from success or in the throes of love are not usually keen to analyse their feelings.

And it is not just feelings of which all this is true. If I start monitoring the attention that I pay when I am driving, I am no longer attending fully to the road and its motoring hazards. But I can reflect later on my level of attention, or someone else can monitor it at the time, without affecting that attention.

Further Reading

Richard Moran, 'Impersonality, character, and moral expressivism', *Journal of Philosophy*, 1993, vol. 90.

The Paradox of the Ravens (Confirmation)

> (R) 'All ravens are black' is logically equivalent to (R–) 'Nothing which is not black is a raven'. A white pen confirms (R–), but surely it does not confirm (R), although (R) says the same as (R–).

To say that (R) is logically equivalent to (R–) is to say that in every possible situation in which one is true so is the other. (R–), which is known as the 'contrapositive' of (R), has the same content as (R), at least in all respects which are relevant here. A generalization like (R) 'All ravens are black' is supported by finding confirming instances of black ravens. And accordingly it would seem that (R–) 'Nothing which is not black is a raven' is supported by confirming instances of things which are neither black nor ravens, like white pens. But a white pen does not seem to support 'All ravens are black'. Most of the things we see are neither ravens nor black. Does each of them really add to our support for this generalization?

One response, that of Carl Hempel who devised the paradox (first published in *Mind* in 1945), is to insist that a white pen *does* confirm (R) in that it gives it *some* support: 'confirmation', as the term is used in confirmation theory, is not understood in terms of conclusive, or even strong, evidence, it is merely a matter of support. The trouble is, it seems, that a white pen should confirm (R–) to the same extent as it confirms (R), and at first sight it does not. But consider how best to find support for (R–). Looking at things which are not black will not get you very far, since they are so numerous and varied. Compare 'Nothing which doesn't have two legs is a man'. You could look at thousands of things without two legs without coming across a one-legged man, despite the fact that there are men with one leg. The best way to confirm (R–) would be to look for ravens and see what colour they were, since there are far fewer ravens than non-ravens.

So the assumption that the best way to confirm generalizations of the form 'All As are B' is always to find confirming instances, instances of As which are B, is untenable. This is particularly obvious in a case like 'All ravens live outside Rutland'. Far from confirming this statement, the sighting of ravens outside Rutland, particularly in adjoining counties with similar climate and environs, would tend to *disconfirm* it. Unless we find some special reason for excluding them from Rutland, the more pervasive their presence in surrounding areas the less likely they are to be absent from that tiny English county. The unreliability of enumerative induction was dramatically illustrated by Bertrand Russell with his example of the chicken whose neck is wrung. We can imagine the chicken fed day after day by the farmer. As the days go by the chicken's expectation that it will be fed every day grows firmer – until one day the farmer comes and wrings its neck.

In short, confirmation is not a simple matter of enumerative induction, that is, the mere accumulation of confirming instances. In particular, we need to take account of other background knowledge. In the case of ravens' colour, this background knowledge will include the fact that birds' plumage serves to protect their species by camouflaging them – otherwise they would have been killed off in the struggle for survival. So it is more important to look for ravens in different environments – temperate, tropical, snowy – than to accumulate more evidence about ravens in our own environment. If we just look at ravens in our own part of the world, then for all we know the species might be dimorphous and come in two different colours: black in temperate regions, white in polar ones. And, once relevant background knowledge is taken into account, any apparent difference in confirmation between (R) and its contrapositive will tend to disappear.

See also **Grue**.

Further Reading

Carl Hempel, *Aspects of Scientific Explanation and Other Essays in the Philosophy of Science*, New York, the Free Press, [1945] 1965.

Bertrand Russell, *Problems of Philosophy*, Oxford, Oxford University Press, [1912] 1959. The chicken example appears in chapter 6, p. 35.

R. M. Sainsbury, *Paradoxes*, 3rd edn, Cambridge, Cambridge University Press, 2009, pp. 95–8.

Richard Swinburne, *An Introduction to Confirmation Theory*, London, Methuen, 1973.

The Red Taxi Paradox

While Mrs Smith is driving at night a taxi comes towards her
and she has to swerve to avoid it. Her legs are broken as a result
of hitting a parked car. The town has only two taxi companies,
the Red Company with red cabs and the Green Company with
green cabs. 60% of the taxis are red. Mrs. Smith saw that
she was hit by a taxi but not which colour it was. She sues the
Red company. We assume the two companies have equally
competent drivers, and that on the evening in question the
journeys of both red and green taxis are distributed evenly
through the city and the 60/40 proportion applies.

In order to win, the claimant must establish the guilt of the
defendant *on the balance of probability*. But although 60%
satisfies this criterion, it is doubtful that she should succeed in
this case (and in Anglo–American law would not succeed).

The hypothetical is inspired by the case of *Smith v. Rapid Transit,
Inc. Mass.* (1945). Betty Smith was driving at night when a bus
forced her to swerve and hit a parked car. She sued Rapid Transit,
Inc. for damages for the injury it caused her. The bus didn't stop
and, while trying to avoid the collision, she saw only that it was a
bus. Rapid Transit was the only company licensed to operate on
that street. But it was held that there was no 'direct' evidence that
the bus belonged to that company, and Mrs Smith lost her case.

The problem involved is more clearly illustrated by the
hypothetical. Is this like the case where I have one lottery ticket out
of 1,000? Arguably I don't know that I will lose, though I know it
is 99.9% probable that I will. Similarly the jury don't know the
taxi was red. But then all they need to know is that it is more likely

than not that the Red Company is at fault, and it seems they know it is 60% probable. So what is missing in Red Taxi for those who doubt Mrs. Smith should succeed? Thomson claims that what is needed is not statistical but 'individualized' evidence that the taxi is red, evidence which requires a causal connection. There is no evidence that causally relates the colour of the taxi to the evidence Mrs Smith is able to present, and it would be a matter of luck for the claimant that it was red. It would have been different if she had seen the colour, say, or if the taxi had grazed her car and left a red patch on it.

Other considerations also count against awarding damages to Mrs Smith. The jury may not fix their subjective probability of its ownership by the Red Company simply according to the 60% proportion. They may think the claimant would have had better evidence in the circumstances.

If the Red Company is held liable in this case, it should in consistency be held liable in similar cases. This is surely unfair to the defendants, who would probably only be at fault in about 60% of the cases. Admittedly companies will insure against such claims, but the Red Company's premiums are likely to be higher than the Green Company's in these circumstances, and that is unfair.

If Green Company is never held liable in such cases but the Red Company is, the Green Company would be less concerned to ensure their men drove carefully, so that there would be more traffic incidents involving taxis (as Richard Posner argues). But this is a consequentialist side-effect.

More importantly, tort law seeks corrective justice: one of its main functions is to compensate for harm, and it is unfair if claimants never get compensation in such cases. One solution would be to award damages proportionately, so that the claimant gets 60% from the Red Company and 40% from the Green. Indeed, the proportions reflect the relative risk to which the companies have exposed the public.

Further Reading

Judith Jarvis Thomson, 'Liability and individualized evidence', in William Parent, ed., *Rights, Restitution, and Risk*, Cambridge Mass. and London, Harvard University Press, 1986.

See also pp. 1378–83 of Charles Nesson, 'The evidence or the event? On judicial proof and the acceptability of verdicts,' *Harvard Law Review*, 1985, vol. 98.

Richard's Paradox

> The set of real numbers definable in a finite number of words is denumerable. But then we can describe in finitely many words another real number formed from an enumeration of the members of this set. So there is a real number that is defined in the enumeration if and only if it isn't.

This paradox was published by Jules Richard in 1905.

A set is denumerable if and only if its members can be paired off one-to-one with the positive integers – for an explanation see **Galileo's Paradox**.

The finitely definable reals (decimal fractions) are enumerable, that is, they can be ordered so that there is a first one, a second, a third, . . . , and in general after each number there is a next. Their definitions can, for example, be grouped according to the number of words used, in ascending order, and ordered alphabetically within each group. Then, in terms of the enumeration of the numbers defined, it is possible to define another real number which is not already included, by means of a procedure due to Cantor which is known as 'diagonalization'. The new number is defined by saying that its nth digit differs from the nth digit of the nth number by replacing it with the next digit up, or by '0' if it is '9'. So if, for example, the 23rd digit of the 23rd number in the enumeration is '7' then it is replaced by '8'. Since this number differs from each of the numbers in the enumeration at one decimal place, it must be distinct from each of them.

Poincaré (1854–1912), one of the pioneer intuitionists, resolved Richard's paradox by means of his 'vicious circle principle', which he thought solved similar paradoxes too, and which came to be espoused by Bertrand Russell. The principle does not allow you to define a totality in terms of itself. The total definable reals cannot therefore include a number defined in terms of that total, and paradox is avoided.

The vicious circle principle has not been generally accepted, however. Gödel pointed out that in classical mathematics there are real numbers definable only in terms of all the real numbers, and, since Gödel thought of the totality of reals as existing independently of us, he saw nothing wrong with such definitions. The totalities are already there to be referred to, so to speak.

If real numbers existed only as human constructions, then there could be no totality which included a member which already presupposed the existence of that totality, since then we would have to have constructed it before we could construct it! We can, however, define the new number and form *another* total, which includes all the numbers in the original enumeration and the new number formed by diagonalization. *Finitely definable real* can then be treated as an 'indefinitely extensible' notion rather than one which is determinate and fixed from the start. (Compare Dummett's approach to **Russell's Paradox**.)

It was thinking about Richard's paradox that actually led Gödel to his celebrated incompleteness theorem (see the final paragraph of the entry on **The Liar**), via realizing that truth could not be defined in arithmetic.

See also **Berry's Paradox**.

Further Reading

*Peter Clark, 'Poincaré, Richard's paradox and indefinite extensibility', *Proceedings of the Philosophy of Science Association*, 1994, vol. 2.

Russell's Paradox

Most of the sets (classes) you are likely to think of will not be members of themselves: the set of whole numbers is not a whole number, the set of nations is not a nation and the set of Frenchwomen is not a Frenchwoman. But the set of everything which is not a Frenchwoman is a member of itself, since it is not a Frenchwoman; so is the set of sets, since it is a set. However, the set of those sets which are not members of themselves is both self-membered and not self-membered.

A set or class is a collection of elements. Those elements belong to the set and are known as its members, and those members may themselves be sets. Clearly the set of Frenchwomen is not a member of itself: what determines this is whether or not the set has its defining property, the property of being a Frenchwoman. The set of sets, on the other hand, does seem to be a member of itself, since it is a set.

Now is the set of the non-self-membered sets – call it R – a member of itself? It cannot belong to R, since then it would not be non-self-membered. But since it does not belong to itself it must belong to the set of non-self-membered sets, R. So it both belongs to R and does not belong to R. Contradiction.

What should determine whether R is a member of itself or not is whether R has its own defining property, which is a matter of whether it is a member of itself. So there would be no independent ground for its (non-)self-membership. And, although the set of the *self*-membered sets doesn't generate a contradiction in the same way, it is equally ungrounded; whether it belongs to itself depends on whether it belongs to itself. All we can do is put the same question again – ad infinitum: the set is ungrounded, because there is no independent factor to determine its status.

So there can be no such sets. But we can't stop there, since it now becomes problematic what a set is, if the unqualified comprehension principle, according to which every predicate determines a set (such and such a set consists of those things of which '*F*' may be predicated), has to be rejected. And for Frege (1848–1925), who was trying to provide logical foundations for arithmetic, the discovery of the paradox was quite traumatic. 'What is in question is not just my particular way of establishing arithmetic', he wrote in a letter to Russell, 'but whether arithmetic can possibly be given a logical foundation at all'.

The Cumulative Hierarchy of Sets

Bertrand Russell (1872–1970) discovered the paradox in 1901, originally formulating it in terms of predicates rather than sets. He struggled hard for several years to find a way of rebuilding the foundations of mathematics free of contradiction, and eventually settled for a complicated 'theory of types'. But a more elegant and natural approach was incorporated in an axiom system by Ernst Zermelo, who had independently discovered Russell's paradox. It was subsequently refined by Abraham Fraenkel and called ZF, and is today the most popular form of axiomatic set theory. In effect it axiomatizes what is known as the 'cumulative hierarchy' or 'iterative conception' of sets. We can gain some understanding of this conception without having to go into what an axiomatic set theory is or into the details of the axioms.

Let an *individual* be anything which is not a set – a person, a plate, a city, a dog, and so on. Stage 0 sets are all the possible sets of individuals. They will include the set of all individuals, probably an infinite set, and all its subsets, including the null set. (The null set is the empty set, the set with no members. See the entry on **Cantor's Paradox** for further explanation.) To qualify as a member of a Stage 1 set an element must be either an individual or a Stage 0 set: so Stage 1 sets include all the Stage 0 sets as well as many more. To qualify as a member of a Stage 2 set an element must be an individual, a Stage 0 set or a Stage 1 set: so Stage 2 sets include all those from Stage 1 and many more. In general a stage includes all the sets from previous stages and admits further sets which may have among their members sets of the last stage. (Actually, set theorists prefer to work with a more abstract version of the hierarchy, which omits the individuals; but we may ignore that here, since it is irrelevant to the resolution of the paradox.)

Stage 0 . . . sets of individuals

Stage 1 . . . sets all of whose members are individuals or Stage 0 sets

Stage 2 . . . sets all of whose members are individuals, Stage 0 sets, or Stage 1 sets

   :

Stage n . . . sets all of whose members are individuals, Stage 0 sets, Stage 1 sets, . . . , or Stage $n-1$ sets

   :

Although the full hierarchy goes on up into mind-boggling 'transfinite' stages, it is enough to consider these simpler stages to see that you will never get a set which belongs to itself. And although as you go up the stages the sets can get more and more comprehensive, since no set can belong to itself you will never get a set of all the sets, nor will you ever get a set of all the non-self-membered sets.

Hypersets

The standard ways of coping with Russell's paradox, type theory and the cumulative hierarchy, exclude all self-membered sets. On these approaches you cannot say of a set that it belongs to itself or that it does not: such assertions are dismissed as having no sense. At first sight this might seem attractive. We have a primitive idea of taking some things and forming a collection of them, but the idea that the collection itself might be one of the things we are collecting together seems bizarre. However, the considerations of the two opening paragraphs above do not rule out *all* self-membered sets. Since the notion of a set can be refined mathematically in various different ways, it is perhaps largely a matter of convenience and elegance which approach we choose, and in these respects ZF is generally regarded as winning out. However, if we want to get to the root of the paradox, it may be a mistake to contend that it stems simply from allowing sets to belong to themselves, just as it is a mistake to think that The Liar paradox stems solely from acknowledging sentences that refer to themselves. And indeed the notion of set can be developed in such a way as to admit self-membered sets (among what are called 'hypersets') without admitting the contradictory Russell set of all non-self-membered sets. The axiom of ZF which bars self-membered sets, the axiom of foundation, is replaced in the version of set theory that admits hypersets by its negation, but the other axioms remain.

The approaches covered so far may banish Russell's paradox, but can we be sure that no other subtler set-theoretic paradox does not import a contradiction somewhere? No, we cannot prove mathematically that this is not so; rather, belief that contradiction has been totally banished is a matter of faith based on happy experience. Gödel showed that it is not possible formally to prove within that system that a formal system (a system where it is decidable whether a formula is a postulate) rich enough for the development of arithmetic is free of contradiction, but it has been shown that the alternative theory admitting hypersets is free of contradiction if ZF is.

An Intuitionist Approach

Michael Dummett calls the discovery of paradoxes like Russell's 'one of the most profound conceptual discoveries of all time, fully worthy to rank with the discovery of irrational numbers' (*The Seas of Language*, p. 440).

Dummett's claim arises from an intuitionist approach, which has its source in Poincaré (1906). What the set-theoretic paradoxes (which also include **Cantor's** and **Richard's**) are supposed to show is that there are 'indefinitely extensible concepts'. Cantor's proof showed that there was no denumerable totality of real numbers (since there are as many real numbers in the interval (0, 1], say, as there are members of the power set of integers – see **The Paradox of Plurality** for a proof). But on the intuitionist view this does not mean that there is a *non-denumerable totality* of all the real numbers. We can go on to construct more and more real numbers, but this is an indefinitely extending collection. Similarly, we can start with a class, C_1, none of whose members belong to themselves, which cannot, on pain of contradiction, contain itself. But then we can go on to form a class, C_2, containing all the members of the first class and C_1 itself. C_2 is not contradictory. Neither is C_3, which contains C_2, and all the members of C_2. And so on. On this so-called constructivist picture we can construct a set of all the non-self-membered sets already constructed, but until it is 'constructed' it is not available to be a member of a set itself. When it is, it is to other sets that it will belong. Non-self-membered sets do not, as it were, already exist to belong to a set of all the non-self-membered sets there are.

As Dummett himself acknowledges, 'the adoption of this solution has a steep price, which most mathematicians would be unwilling to pay: the rejection of classical methods of argument in mathematics in favour of constructive ones' (p. 442). However, it may be possible to construe indefinite extensibility in a non-constructivist way.

See also **Cantor's Paradox, Richard's Paradox**, as well as those in the liar group: **The Liar, Curry's Paradox, Yablo's Paradox, Heterological, Berry's Paradox**.

Further Reading

*George Boolos, 'The iterative conception of set', in Paul Benacerraf and Hilary Putnam, eds, *Philosophy of Mathematics*, 2nd edn, 1983, reprinted in his *Logic, Logic, and Logic*, Cambridge, Mass., Harvard University Press, 1999.

*Michael Dummett, *The Seas of Language*, Oxford, Clarendon Press, 1993, pp. 440–45.

*R. M. Sainsbury, *Paradoxes*, 3rd edn, Cambridge, Cambridge University Press, 2009, section 1.

For a good introductory account of constructivism, see *Stephen Read, *Thinking about Logic*, Oxford, Oxford University Press, 1995, chapter 8.

The St Petersburg Paradox

A fair coin is tossed until it lands Heads up. If this happens on the nth throw the bank pays the player £2^n. The expected or average gain is therefore infinite, and, whatever sum the player pays to play she has the advantage.

This needs some explanation. Suppose you are the player: if Heads comes up on the first throw you get £2, if it comes up on the second throw you get £4, on the third £8, and so on. For each successive throw the payout doubles. The chance of heads on the first throw is $\frac{1}{2}$; the chance that heads comes up first on the second throw is the chance of Tails on the first × $\frac{1}{2}$, that is, $\frac{1}{4}$; the chance that Heads comes up first on the third throw is $\frac{1}{2} \times \frac{1}{2} \times \frac{1}{2}$, and so on. For each successive throw the chance halves, just as the payout doubles. The expected gain from the first toss is £2 × the probability that it is Heads ($\frac{1}{2}$), that is, £1; from the second throw it is £4 × $\frac{1}{4}$ = £1; from the third £8 × $\frac{1}{8}$ = £1, and in general for the nth throw it is £2^n × $\frac{1}{2^n}$ = £1. Since there is no limit to the possible number of throws before Heads comes up, the sum for the expected gains, $1 + 1 + 1 + \ldots$ goes on for ever and the expectation is infinite. Yet would you pay *any* sum, however large, to participate?

(1) Any real bank has finite resources. But this evades the theoretical challenge to the notion of expectation. Anyway, we can still consider what the bank owes and count that as to the player's credit.

(2) It was to explain away the St Petersburg paradox that Daniel Bernouilli devised the notion of diminishing returns.

Suppose you start off earning £700 a month, and in successive months get a rise of £100 a month. At first the rise has considerable value for you, but a few years later when you are earning £8,000 a month the extra £100 is of much less value to you: the returns from the £100 increments diminish as you get more and more of them.

So it appears that, owing to diminishing returns, a gain of £2 billion will not have twice the utility of a gain of £1 billion. When you already have £1 billion, what can you spend your second billion on that will add to your life as much as the first billion? But we can set aside diminishing returns in the St Petersburg game by construing utility more broadly. When you win more than you can spend for your own personal consumption there remains unlimited scope for philanthropy. As Bertrand put it, 'Does there exist no family that [you] may enrich or no misery [you] may relieve, are there no great works that [you] may create or cause to be created?'

In any case, there is a way of strengthening the paradox so that the payouts allow for diminishing returns while the expected utility, even construed selfishly, is still infinite.

(3) A third response to the paradox explains our unwillingness to pay a huge stake in terms of risk aversion. It is rational to stake £10 for a 20 per cent chance of winning £100, but some people are not prepared to risk losing their money: they are risk-averse. (Those addicted to gambling tend to be the opposite, and to be attracted to unprofitable risks.) But is risk aversion rational?

A case can be made for risk aversion in certain cases – cases where we are practically certain to lose, no matter how favourable the expected utility. Would you stake £10,000 for one chance in a million of £20 billion (i.e. twenty thousand million)? You are almost certain to lose your £10,000, and, unless you are very rich and would not notice the loss, it would seem a foolish gamble. If you would take that risk, would you risk £10,000 for a one in a billion chance of £20,000 billion? A one in a billion chance is so tiny that you might as well discount it completely. For the bank there is a risk attraction, since it will happily accept your £10,000 if its risk of ruin is so tiny as to be ignored. The 'Sure Loss Principle' advises players not to take the risk of any significant loss if that loss is almost certain, however great the expected utility of taking it. Here is a decision principle, then, which clashes with the principle of maximizing expected utility. (See Jordan, cited below.) But even if the Sure Loss Principle were not rationally defensible, its appeal would provide a psychological explanation of our unwillingness to pay a huge stake in the St Petersburg game. (See **Allais' Paradox** under (4).)

We can distinguish two aspects of the paradox. One is the fact that there are huge sums that no one would pay despite the infinite expected utility for the player. This paradox does not depend on the infinite expectation, since as seen above it arises in cases where the finite expectation is large because there is a tiny chance of an enormous win.

The other aspect is the impossibility of a fair game, and this does depend on the infinite expectation. For it remains the case that there is no 'fair' single St Petersburg game, nor is there a fair sequence of games if the stake is the same for each game and is not a function of the number of games. But if every time you play a new game the fee for each of the games you have played rises according to a certain formula, the player's advantage disappears, and with it the paradox. (The formula and its proof are given in Feller, pp. 251–53.) A single St Petersburg game or a multiple St Petersburg game where the stake per game does not vary according to the number of games is paradoxical, and, bewildering though it may seem, no such game can be fair. This seems to be one of those paradoxes which we have to swallow.

The paradox was discovered by Nicolaus Bernouilli, and acquired its name because it was first published in an article by Daniel Bernouilli in the St Petersburg Academy Proceedings in 1738.

Further Reading

Jeff Jordan, 'The St. Petersburg paradox and Pascal's Wager', *Philosophia*, 1994, vol. 23.

Maurice Kraitchik, *Mathematical Recreations*, London, Allen & Unwin, 1943, pp. 135–39.

For fair multiple games see: *William Feller, *An Introduction to Probability*, New York, John Wiley, 1968, pp. 251–53.

The Self-Amendment Paradox

If a constitutional rule provides for the amendment of the constitution in accordance with certain specified conditions, it would seem to be impossible to amend the rule itself legitimately. Yet this is surely contrary to accepted legal practice.

Consider Article V of the US Constitution:

> The Congress, whenever two thirds of both Houses shall deem it necessary, shall propose Amendments to this Constitution, or, on the Application of the Legislatures of two thirds of the several States, shall call a Convention for proposing Amendments, which, in either Case, shall be valid to all Intents and Purposes, as Part of this Constitution, when ratified by the Legislatures of three fourths of the several States, or by Conventions in three fourths thereof, as the one or the other Mode of Ratification may be proposed by the Congress . . .

The Article partly refers to itself, since it is part of the Constitution for which it is providing conditions of amendment. The Scandinavian legal realist Alf Ross argues that partial self-reference in propositions is no better than total self-reference, which he thinks deprives them of meaning. Such an article may not be amended by the legal process it prescribes, since partial self-reference renders it meaningless in so far as it is self-referential.

In self-referring instances of 'This proposition is false' or 'This proposition is true' there is contradiction or vacuity. 'This sentence expresses a false proposition', if it said anything, would be false if and only if true, and 'This sentence expresses a true proposition' has nothing to determine whether it is true or false – it is an idle cog. In the latter case we would need to determine whether it was true before we could determine whether it was true. (See the Liar.) Hart regards (2) in the list

(1) Grass is green,
(2) Every statement in this list is true including this one,

as unobjectionable. But (2) can be consistently regarded as false as well as true, and so there is nothing to determine its truth value. In this respect it is like the self-referential instance of 'This proposition is true'. It may well be that partially self-referring propositions which ascribe nothing but truth or falsity are always problematic.

Nevertheless, propositional self-reference is sometimes admissible. Consider, for example, an informal interpretation of the famous Gödelian formula:

(G) This proposition, G, is not provable in Peano Arithmetic,

which is true if Peano Arithmetic is consistent.

But there is no good reason why Article V cannot itself be amended on application of two thirds of the States and ratification by three quarters of them. Ross argues that, if it were meaningful, then the new amendment arising out of the provisions of the article would be logically contrary to the article itself. Indeed, it couldn't be otherwise if the original article is being amended. But this provides no difficulty, because there is no logical contradiction in a situation in which the article applies until it is amended and a new, amended article applies after that.

Ross also considers an alternative explanation: that any amendment of a partially self-referring provision is simply the 'outcome of socio-psychological fact' (p. 18). He rightly rejects this on the grounds that it does not genuinely reflect legal practice.

He thinks we need to add a basic norm N_0. Applied to the Article V it would read: 'Obey the authority instituted by Art. V, until this authority itself points out a successor; then obey this authority, until it itself points out a successor; and so on indefinitely' (cf. p. 24). But this basic norm is unnecessary. Just as the rules for an institution do not need to have an additional rule, 'Obey these rules', to make them binding, Article V does not need Ross's basic norm in order to be applicable to itself. It authorizes its own amendment without such assistance.

Further Reading

H. L. A. Hart, 'Self-referring laws', 1964, repr. in his *Essays in Jurisprudence and Philosophy*, Oxford, Clarendon Press, 1983.

Alf Ross, 'On self-reference and a puzzle in constitutional law', *Mind*, 1969, vol. 78.

Peter Suber, 'The paradox of self-amendment in constitutional law', *Stanford Literature Review*, 1990, vol. 7, pp. 53–78.

Self-deception

I can be a victim of another's deception but I can also be a victim of self-deception. You cannot succeed in deceiving me if I know what you are up to. So how can I deceive myself? Won't I know what I am up to, and won't this necessarily undermine the self-deception?

This paradox has led some philosophers into denying that there is such a phenomenon as self-deception, but human self-deception is so undeniably a feature of human life that one is tempted to say they are deceiving themselves in the interests of philosophical simplicity.

If I deliberately deceive you, then I intentionally mislead you. So how can I deceive myself? Won't I know what I am up to, and won't that defeat the attempt to deceive? Belief is not directly under the control of the will: I can't just voluntarily change my belief. So how can I trick myself into believing otherwise? Can I do so only by leaving false clues for myself in the hope that they will mislead me later? It doesn't seem that ordinary cases of self-deception are like that.

It is commonplace that our desires and emotions influence our beliefs without the mediation of intention. Thus, if I am in a good mood I will tend to be optimistic, to believe that things will turn out well; and when my wife is angry she will tend to notice my faults rather than my virtues. Someone disappointed because her son has been rejected for a coveted position may become more alive to the drawbacks of the job and less to its advantages ('sour grapes'). Of course, the emotions are often produced by beliefs, but that does not mean that emotions do not themselves induce beliefs, as our experience constantly attests. Extraordinarily, it has been

224

claimed that emotions and moods can be produced by beliefs but not vice versa. But this is belied by the way in which highly optimistic attitudes and beliefs are produced by drug-induced euphoria, and deeply pessimistic ones by drug-induced depression.

'Fere libenter homines id quod volunt credunt', wrote Caesar. ('In general people willingly believe what they want to.') For example, according to a recent survey, 94 per cent of American academics considered themselves more competent than their average colleague. Some self-deception seems to be a form of wishful thinking. Nor do we need to form a plan to trick ourselves: our desires and emotions, our self-esteem, impel us to look partially and dishonestly at the evidence that presents itself. A mother knows her young son was burnt through her negligence in leaving him unsupervised for a while, but would rather think she was not responsible for it. The mother concentrates on how short a time the child was alone. She was in the kitchen and was keeping an eye on her son through the door, wasn't she? You can't be watching a child every second, these accidents are impossible to avoid, and the burn wasn't really that extensive. She bandages it up and doesn't look at it too closely. She lets her neighbour comfort her, hearing how the neighbour's child has just fallen and broken its leg. Negligence is lack of *reasonable* care, and she exercised reasonable care, didn't she?

It is common enough, in any case, for people to draw hasty conclusions from imperfect evidence, to misinterpret evidence, to attend to it selectively through ignorance or impatience. The definition of a human being as a *rational animal* was always over-optimistic. Add strong motivation, a deep reluctance to face certain facts, and a fervent desire to protect or enhance our self-esteem, and we are all the more prone not to accept what may be staring us in the face unless it suits us to do so. So a belief may be formed dishonestly or a pre-existing belief may be dishonestly retained.

Not all self-deception is a form of wishful thinking, however. Sometimes we are self-deceived in believing what we fear, as when a possessive lover is inclined too readily to believe the loved one is unfaithful. It is understandable that he should pay especial attention to signs of possible infidelity, and this sensitivity may help him to take measures against the realization of his fear. Or the self-deception may simply be a symptom of low self-esteem, just as wish-fulfilling self-deception may sometimes be a symptom of excess of it.

Some writers claim that an appeal to intention is necessary to explain why some desires and fears lead to self-deception and others do not. And no doubt there are also other forms of self-deception in which we really know what in another part of our mind we refuse to accept. Perhaps I know unconsciously or subconsciously that my business is failing and, through subconscious mechanisms, have induced at the fully conscious level a belief that it is not. Much has been hypothesized on these lines, some of it inspired by Freud. It would be a mistake to assume in advance of investigation that there is only one type of self-deception: the existence of self-deception of the sorts sketched above does not preclude another species of self-deception involving some sort of mental compartmentalizing.

There are cases, then, where selective attention induced by our desires and fears enables us to hide from ourselves what we are up to, so that our self-deception is not undermined. If in addition there is unconsciously motivated self-deception, then it is in the nature of the case that what we are up to is hidden from us. But if there are cases of self-deception in which we have intentions to deceive ourselves that are not unconscious, then these will be generally more difficult to explain, though no doubt selective attention will play an important part in these too.

Further Reading

J. Bermúdez, 'Self-deception, intentions, and contradictory beliefs', *Analysis*, 2000, vol. 60.

T. S. Champlin, *Reflexive Paradoxes*, London, Routledge, 1988.

Jean-Pierre Dupuy, ed., *Self-deception and Paradoxes of Rationality*, Stanford, California, CSLI Publications, 1998.

Alfred R. Mele, *Self-deception Unmasked*, Princeton, NJ, and Oxford, Princeton University Press, 2001.

David Pears, *Motivated Irrationality*, New York, OUP, 1984.

Self-fulfilling Belief

If I believe that I am believing this, where 'this' refers to that very belief, my belief necessarily makes itself true. But I cannot hold this as a belief, since it has no genuine content.

Some beliefs are self-fulfilling – true because they are believed. It is in virtue of such beliefs that placebos work: I believe the pills I have been prescribed will cure me, and that very belief effects the cure, since the pill itself is pharmacologically inert. If shareholders believe that share prices are going to rise, they will buy shares in the hope of selling them later at a profit, thereby raising share prices and making their belief true.

Of course, unwitting belief about placebos and beliefs in bull markets do not always fulfil themselves. But it might be thought that there is one belief that you can have that is bound to make itself true, namely the belief that you are believing, that is, the belief (B) that you are believing B. Such a belief would be self-verifying, just as saying 'I am speaking English' makes itself true by the very utterance of the words.

The trouble is that the beliefs that the pill will make you better or that shares will rise have a content: there is something that you believe. But does B have a genuine content? In the other cases believing is not the same as what you believe, but in the case of B the believing is its own content. What is this B you are believing? we may ask. The answer that I am believing B may seem no answer at all. At the very least we have a degenerate case of belief, if it can count as a case of belief at all. And if we don't have a case of genuine belief here, B is not a case of self-fulfilling belief after all.

Putative belief in B is like saying (S), 'This is a statement', where 'this' is meant to refer to S itself, or asking (Q) 'Is this a question?', where Q is meant to refer to Q itself. Arguably the first is not a genuine piece of stating, since there is nothing it states, unless it is taken to mean that the utterance has the grammatical form of an assertive sentence. Similarly, you fail really to ask anything in asking whether (Q) is a question, unless this is taken as asking whether the sentence has the interrogative form in grammar.

For a paradox of self-frustrating belief see The Placebo Paradox.

Further Reading

Peter Cave, 'Too self-fulfilling', *Analysis*, 2001, vol. 61.

The Ship of Theseus

> Over a period of years, in the course of maintenance a ship has its planks replaced one by one – call this ship A. However, the old planks are retained and themselves reconstituted into a ship – call this ship B. At the end of this process there are two ships. Which one is the original ship of Theseus?

This is another famous puzzle about identity and material constitution. It was discussed by the great seventeenth century political philosopher Thomas Hobbes (1588–1679) in his *De Corpore* (Part 2, Chapter 11, section 7). The history of Theseus' ship was originally recounted by Plutarch (*c*. 46–*c*. 120).

If the old planks had been discarded or just left in a pile, we should have had only one ship. And despite its changing constitution it would have retained its identity: Theseus' ship would have remained continuously in existence. If a mere change of a plank meant that the ship had been replaced by another one, very few things would last more than a split second. *We* wouldn't, for example, since our molecular constitution is constantly changing little by little. Even a major change like the loss of both legs need not destroy a person or that person's body.

But what if we have the reconstituted ship, B, as well? Until it is largely reconstituted we still have only one ship, which does not suffer any break in its continuity. If the reconstituted ship is identical with the original, when did A, the ship which had its planks replaced, cease to be the original ship? Did the original ship suddenly switch to becoming the reconstituted one or was there a break in continuity? These problems are not, however, an insuperable difficulty for the option that B is the same as the original ship, A. For there need be no determinate time at which the switch occurs, any more than there is any determinate time, except in law, at which a child becomes an adult. As for discontinuity, if I completely dismantle my car and then put it together again, I still have my original car. Even so, it seems more natural to identify A with Theseus' original ship in the situation we have described.

However, a context can be described in which it would be more natural to make this claim for B. Suppose Theseus' original ship is getting rather dilapidated and needs a thorough overhaul. He decides to take each plank out, repair it, and put the planks together again to restore his ship: this will be B. But it takes time, because he cannot afford much help. Nor can he afford to be without marine transport. So when he takes a plank out he replaces it with a cheap piece of wood, so that he continues to have some sort of ship to travel in for temporary use: this is A. At the end of this process would it not then be more natural to regard B as his original ship, now newly restored and fully seaworthy?

Perhaps there is no right answer to this question of identity. In some contexts one answer may seem more compelling or convenient, in others the other answer. But there is no mystery about what has happened. So perhaps it does not really matter whether it is A or B that we identify with Theseus' original ship.

However, appealing as it may seem, this quietist approach has its problems. Suppose Theseus had insured his ship before the planks were replaced. Which ship is insured after the reconstitution: A or B? Is the insurance company now liable for accidental damage to ship B? Some would say that there is no determinate answer to this question until a court of law has pronounced on it. Yet if an appeal court makes a judgment on the matter it will claim to be ruling on what the law is, rather than to be legislating anew; legislation is the job of Parliament, not the judiciary.

See also **Heraclitus' Paradox.**

Further Reading

David Wiggins, *Sameness and Substance Renewed*, Cambridge, Cambridge University Press, 2001.

Simpson's Paradox

Although one hospital has better overall survival rates for surgery for a given condition than another, it doesn't follow that you will improve your chances of survival by choosing to go to the one with the better overall record.

Here are comparative data for surgery for a particular condition at two hospitals:

	Survived	Died	Total	Survival rate
Mercy Hospital	750	250	1000	75%
Charity Hospital	840	160	1000	84%

If you had the condition in question, which hospital would you prefer for surgery? Charity seems the obvious choice. But now look at the figures when they are disaggregated to take into account whether patients are in good condition or bad condition before surgery:

For patients initially in good condition the results are:

Good condition	Survived	Died	Total	Survival rate
Mercy Hospital	490	10	500	98%
Charity Hospital	810	90	900	90%

For patients initially in bad condition the results are:

Bad condition	Survived	Died	Total	Survival rate
Mercy Hospital	260	240	500	52%
Charity Hospital	30	70	100	30%

233

Whether you are in good condition or bad, your prospects now seem better at Mercy Hospital.

How could this be? The critical factor is your prior condition. As you would expect, if it is good, then your prospects are much better than if it is bad. If a hospital's success rate is higher for those in good condition than those in bad, as it is for both of the hospitals in the example above, then the higher the proportion of those it treats who are in good condition the higher its overall success rate. The proportion of patients in good condition who undergo surgery at Charity Hospital is 90 per cent compared with 50 per cent at Mercy. This explains why, on the figures above, the overall success rate of Charity is higher than that of Mercy: it has the easier cases. But its success with both the patients in good condition and those in bad is worse. Go to Mercy rather than Charity if you have the choice.

If the proportion of patients in good condition is the same in both hospitals, then the aggregated table will show more success for Mercy. Given a table of the first sort and overall success rates for patients in good and bad condition respectively you can get a more reliable idea of which hospital is more successful for either kind of patients by 'normalizing' the figures to make the proportions the same in each hospital.

The following chart shows how the overall survival rate in Charity Hospital varies with an increasing proportion of patients in good condition: from 30 per cent if everyone starts off in bad condition to 90 per cent if everyone is in good condition to start with.

The chart also helps to bring out an affinity with **The Xenophobic Paradox (The Medical Test)**, though the latter does not involve disaggregation in the same way and so is simpler.

Disaggregation with respect to the patients' prior condition may not be the end of the matter. There may be other factors which affect survival prospects: age, sex, smoking, exercise, genetic constitution and so on. The problem in investigations of this sort

Proportion in good condition in Charity Hospital

is to know how finely to break down the aggregated figures, and to do that we need to know which factors are causally relevant to the ailment. Much further investigation may be needed.

The example given above is of course merely one instance of Simpson's paradox, which covers many different sorts of cases where aggregation misleads. Just as **The Xenophobic Paradox** has many variants, like the medical test, so does Simpson's paradox.

The paradox dates back to Yu (1903), was introduced to philosophers by Cohen and Nagel in 1934, and discussed in a paper by Simpson in 1951. (See Malinas below for details.)

See also **The Xenophobic Paradox.**

Further Reading

*Maurice H. DeGroot, *Probability and Statistics*, Reading, Mass., Addison-Wesley, 1989.
*Gary Malinas, 'Simpson's paradox and the wayward researcher', *Australasian Journal of Philosophy*, 1997, vol. 75.

The Sleeping Beauty

On Sunday Beauty learns she is going to be put to sleep for the next two days, and be woken briefly either once or twice. A fair coin is tossed: if it lands Heads she will be woken just on Monday, if Tails on both Monday and Tuesday. If she is woken just on Monday, she is put back to sleep with a drug that makes her forget that waking. Beauty knows all this, so that when she wakes on Monday she doesn't know which day it is. On waking, what probability should she assign to the coin having landed Heads?

(1) A half, because it was a fair coin and she's learned nothing new relevant to how it fell.

(2) One-third, because if the trial were repeated week after week, she should expect twice as many Tails-wakings as Heads-wakings. For every time the coin lands Tails she is woken twice, as compared with once when it lands Heads.

At first sight the argument in (2) appears suspect. Consider a similar case where the chance of multiple wakings is much higher. Suppose that Rip van Winkle is treated like the Sleeping Beauty except that if the coin lands Tails he is woken on 999 rather than just two successive days. Then, arguing as in (2), on waking on Monday not knowing which of the 999 days it is, his probability for Heads should be one in a thousand. Can this be right?

When we talk here of the probability you should assign to an event, we mean the degree of belief you should have in it, which is known as your *credence*.

The Sleeping Beauty's credence in Heads when first waking on Monday is the same as her credence in *The coin landed Heads and it's Monday*, because she knows that if it is now Tuesday the coin must have landed Tails. Express this credence as '$P(\text{Heads}_{\text{Monday}})$'.

Now if her credence in Heads should be $\frac{1}{2}$, her credence in Tails should also be $\frac{1}{2}$, not $\frac{2}{3}$ as the second answer would have it. Then, if the coin landed Tails, as far as she is concerned it is as likely to be Monday as Tuesday, so her credence in *It's Monday and the coin landed Tails* [$P(\text{Tails}_{\text{Monday}})$] should be the same as her credence in *It's Tuesday and the coin landed Tails* [$P(\text{Tails}_{\text{Tuesday}})$]. So $P(\text{Tails}_{\text{Monday}}) = P(\text{Tails}_{\text{Tuesday}}) = \frac{1}{4}$.

Whichever answer is correct, the effect of going on to tell Beauty that it is Monday, before she is put to sleep again with the drug, should be that her credence in Heads rises. Call it now 'P_+'.

$P_+(\text{Heads}_{\text{Monday}})$	$P_+(\text{Tails}_{\text{Monday}})$	$P_+(\text{Tails}_{\text{Tuesday}})$

In the figure above, the shaded part is excluded when she is told it is Monday, so that her credence for $P_+(\text{Heads}_{\text{Monday}})$ + $P_+(\text{Tails}_{\text{Monday}}) = 1$.

On being woken up on Monday she knew that it was

$\text{Heads}_{\text{Monday}}$ or $\text{Tails}_{\text{Monday}}$ or $\text{Tails}_{\text{Tuesday}}$.

Let $P(\text{Heads}_{\text{Monday}})$ be her credence in Heads in that situation. When told it is Monday, she knows it is $\text{Heads}_{\text{Monday}}$ or $\text{Tails}_{\text{Monday}}$, and her credence in Heads should rise to $P(\text{Heads}_{\text{Monday}})/$ $(P(\text{Heads}_{\text{Monday}}) + P(\text{Tails}_{\text{Monday}}))$. For example, if $P(\text{Heads}_{\text{Monday}})$ was $\frac{1}{2}$, since $P(\text{Tails}_{\text{Monday}}) = P(\text{Tails}_{\text{Tuesday}}) = \frac{1}{4}$ her credence in Heads should rise to $\frac{1}{2}$ divided by $(\frac{1}{2} + \frac{1}{4})$, which is $\frac{2}{3}$. If the competing view that $P(\text{Heads}_{\text{Monday}})$ is $\frac{1}{3}$ is right, it should rise from $\frac{1}{3}$ to $\frac{1}{3}$ divided by $(\frac{1}{3} + \frac{1}{3})$, that is, to $\frac{1}{2}$.

The problem, which is presented by Adam Elga in the paper cited below, is relevant to decisions under uncertainty, for example in economics. He offers an argument for $P(\text{Heads}_{\text{Monday}}) = \frac{1}{3}$, whereas David Lewis, in the reply cited below, argues for $P(\text{Heads}_{\text{Monday}}) = \frac{1}{2}$, on the ground that on first waking up on

Monday she has learned nothing new relevant to how the coin has landed. On the other hand, when she is told it is Monday she acquires information about the future, 'namely that she is not now in it', which should modify her credence in Heads, ignoring the known chances of Heads = $\frac{1}{2}$ and Tails = $\frac{1}{2}$.

However, there is a competing consideration, which speaks in favour of Elga's view ((2) above). Suppose that whenever she is woken Beauty is offered even odds on the coin having fallen Heads. Then, if immediately on being woken Beauty has a policy of betting on Heads, she is more likely to lose than to win.

The Sleeping Beauty is a variant produced by R. Stalnaker from an example devised by Arnold Zuboff. (See *Inquiry* 1990.) Related problems have been discussed in the literature on game theory.

Further Reading

Adam Elga, 'Self-locating belief and the Sleeping Beauty problem', *Analysis*, 2000, vol. 60.

David Lewis, 'Sleeping Beauty: reply to Elga', *Analysis*, 2001, vol. 61.

The Paradox of Soundness

(A)   This argument, A, is unsound
          _____

          Therefore this argument, A, is unsound

If A is sound, then it is a valid argument with a true premiss; but if its premiss is true it is unsound.

If A is unsound its premiss is true and A is invalid; but it cannot be invalid, since its form is that of the trivially valid 'p, therefore p'. So it must be sound.

Therefore A is both sound and unsound.

This paradox, due to Dale Jacquette, has an obvious affinity with The Paradox of Validity in its various forms.

The same type of reason as given in the entry for that other paradox can be given for treating constituent statements of A as failing to say anything. A (one-premiss) argument is sound in the sense relevant here when its premiss is true and its conclusion follows from that premiss. So to assess the argument for soundness we have to determine whether the premiss is true and whether the argument is valid. But in order to determine whether the premiss is true we have to determine whether the argument is sound. We cannot determine whether it is sound without first determining whether it is sound. So arguably we cannot properly attribute either soundness or unsoundness to the argument, and its constituents are ungrounded. And, if we are not really confronted with a genuine argument, the paradox disappears.

The Spaceship

A spaceship travels in a straight line. It doubles its speed after half a minute, doubles it again after another quarter of a minute, and continues successively to double it after half of the last interval. Where is it at one minute? It is neither infinitely far away, nor at any finite distance either.

It is not infinitely far away, since there is no such place. But it cannot be at any finite distance from its start after one minute, since that would involve an inexplicable spatio-temporal discontinuity in its existence. For in that minute it could not trace a continuous straight-line path through space and time to any point a finite distance from its start if it were to satisfy the description above: any finite distance from the start, however far, is reached before the minute is up.

The only way to avoid this incoherence would be for it to shrink gradually into nothing, say by halving every time it doubled its speed. In any case, if it did not shrink like this, it would have to be travelling infinitely fast at one minute. So the only admissible answer is: nowhere. (If, on the other hand, you allow it to be spatio-temporally discontinuous, it could be anywhere.)

The paradox is an invention of Benardete's.

Further Reading

A. W. Moore, *The Infinite*, 2nd edn, London and New York, Routledge, 2001, chapter 4.

The Toxin Paradox

> You are offered a million dollars to form the intention of drinking a vile potion which, though not lethal, will make you unpleasantly ill. Once you have formed the intention the money is handed over, and you are free to change your mind. The trouble is that you know this, and it will prevent you from forming the intention, since you cannot intend to do what you know you will not do.

We suppose that you are not allowed to arrange that you be bound or forced to fulfil the intention. Nor do you have any other reason to drink once you have the money. So although you had good reason to form the intention, you have no reason to drink the potion once the money is yours. How then can you form the intention? 'I intend to drink the potion but I won't drink it' is as self-defeating a belief or utterance as one of the form 'p but I don't believe it' (see **Moore's Paradox**). Normally your reasons for forming an intention to do A are your reasons for doing A; but in this case they come apart.

There may seem to be no way out here. However, David Gauthier argues that it is rational to adopt a policy of forming intentions and fulfilling them if you will be better off as a result than if you hadn't formed the intentions. What matters here is not whether he is right but whether you can convince yourself of this enough to adopt the policy. If you believe he is right, you can form the intention to drink the toxin and then drink it. You will suffer the unpleasant illness but get the million dollars, which is better than avoiding the illness and not getting the money. If you are not sufficiently persuaded of the merit of the policy to take it on, you will be unable to form the intention, even if Gauthier *is* right about the rationality of the policy.

Compare the **Indy** and **Deterrence Paradoxes**, which are effectively extensions of this one.

Further Reading

David Gauthier, 'Assure and threaten', *Ethics*, 1994, vol. 104.
Gregory Kavka, 'The toxin paradox', *Analysis*, 1983, vol. 43.

The Paradox of Tragedy
(Horror)

'It seems an unaccountable pleasure, which the spectators [of works of tragedy] receive from sorrow, terror, anxiety, and other passions, that are in themselves disagreeable and uneasy. The more they are touched and affected, the more are they delighted with the spectacle ... They are pleased in proportion as they are afflicted, and never so happy as when they employ tears, sobs and cries to give vent to their sorrow.'

(David Hume, 'Of Tragedy')

How can this be? For one thing, Hume is too ready to assert that the negative emotions are disagreeable. Many people enjoy a certain amount of danger and risk and the frisson of anxiety and fear they produce (why else scale mountains or race cars as an amateur?) and there are those who derive a certain satisfaction from sorrow, grief and pity.

But deep sorrow, paralysing terror and obsessive anxiety are highly unpleasant. When the objects are merely fictional, however, these emotional states can be absorbing and gratifying and do not cause the same distress as when their objects are real. We need to distinguish the emotional feelings from the objects of those feelings. The misery or misfortune in the object of pity will not necessarily be reflected in our feelings towards it. When we believe the object is real, natural human sympathy is more likely to make the pity an unpleasant experience, but if the object is known to be fictional we can derive satisfaction from the feeling without lacking sympathy for our fellow human beings. Disgust, on the other hand, is more likely to be unpleasant, even when its object is known to be fictional.

Many people derive aesthetic satisfaction from tragic drama. The interest in the unfolding of a tragic plot is heightened by the emotions, and our attention can be held by both our emotional and our intellectual absorption. And we can even derive comfort from tragedies through imagining people far worse off than we are. It is relevant to the parallel paradox about our responses to works of horror – a genre unknown in Hume's day – that many are fascinated by Gothic weirdness in horror stories and films. All this goes some way towards explaining why tragedy and horror play such a large part in human entertainment.

Those, like Kendall Walton, who resolve the paradox of fiction by regarding our affective responses to fictional objects as quasi-emotions, on the ground that we must believe in the existence of the objects of our genuine emotions, may claim that we can derive satisfaction, even pleasure, from these responses to works of tragedy and horror because those responses are not the true emotions of sorrow, terror, pity or anxiety. Yet, even if we recognize quasi-emotions, that does not of itself provide a resolution of the paradoxes of tragedy and horror, merely a way of restating them, since it will have to be admitted that quasi-emotions feel very much like genuine ones. In any case the entry on **The Paradox of Fiction** offers good reasons for rejecting the view.

Unlike the paradox of fiction, the paradoxes of tragedy and horror are not resolvable in purely philosophical terms but require an appeal to human psychology, which is more complex than the paradox suggests.

See also **The Paradox of Fiction.**

Further Reading

Noël Carroll, *The Philosophy of Horror*, New York and London, Routledge, 1990.

The Tristram Shandy

Tristram Shandy takes two years to cover his first two days in his autobiography. He can continue at the same rate and still finish it if he never dies.

Read **Galileo's Paradox** first.

Even at a constant rate of two years for two days the eponymous hero of Laurence Sterne's novel can cover his whole life if he lives for ever. For each successive pair of days can be paired off exhaustively with each successive pair of years: each two-day period will have its own matching two-year period in which the events of the two days can be written up – though his memory will need to stretch back further and further without end. For example, days 101 and 102 will be written up about a century later in years 101 and 102, and days 1001 and 1002 written up nearly a millennium later.

The paradox is due to Bertrand Russell, who draws an analogy with **Achilles and the Tortoise.** *See also* the essentially similar **Hilbert's Hotel.**

Further Reading

Bertrand Russell, *The Principles of Mathematics*, London, Allen & Unwin, [1903] 1937, pp. 358–60.

The Trojan Fly

Achilles travels at 8 mph but the tortoise manages only 1 mph. So Achilles has given it a start. At the point where Achilles catches the tortoise he draws level with a fly which proceeds to fly back and forth between them at 20 mph. After another hour Achilles is 7 miles ahead of the tortoise, but where is the fly?

It looks as if it should be possible to calculate its position and determine its direction. But the answer is that it could be anywhere, facing either direction.

To see that the fly could be anywhere, imagine the event run backwards. If the fly is placed at any point between the two, facing either direction, and the motions of Achilles and the tortoise are exactly reversed, they will all end up together at the point where Achilles originally overtook the tortoise.

How can the fly get started, since any distance it flies from either Achilles or the tortoise at 20 mph must take it beyond them? But, as with the regressive version of **The Racecourse**, there can be no first interval that the fly travels. There will have to be infinitely many distinct ways in which the fly can proceed, since there are infinitely many distinct destinations it could reach after one hour by flying backwards and forwards between the two runners at 20 mph.

One bizarre feature of the example is that the fly must change direction infinitely often. Indeed, for any moment after the start, however short, it must have changed direction infinitely often. And the example is unreal in assuming that every time the fly changes direction it does so instantaneously.

After A. K. Austin of Sheffield, *Mathematics Magazine*, 1971, adapted by Wesley Salmon.

Further Reading

Wesley C. Salmon, *Space, Time and Motion*, Enrico, California and Belmont, California, Dickenson Publishing Co., Inc., 1975, chapter 2.

The Trolley Problem

> A trolley's brakes have failed and it is careering towards five
> workmen on the track ahead; a bystander can avert their death
> by pulling a lever and diverting the trolley to a spur that forks
> off to the right, though only at the expense of killing a workman
> on the spur. Should he turn the trolley?
>
> While it may be permissible, even mandatory, to divert the
> trolley, it is not in general right to sacrifice one to save many.
> For example, five patients dying from organ failure can be saved
> from death only by transplanting organs from a sixth, healthy
> individual. Should he be sacrificed to save the other five? Surely
> not. But why not?

A well-known example from the Second World War seems morally
akin to Trolley. When rockets started falling on densely populated
London, a proposal was made to deceive the Germans into thinking
they had overshot, so that they would change their aim and make
most of them land on the less densely populated areas of the home
counties. Although Herbert Morrison rejected the proposal, saying
it would be playing God, scientists implemented it with some
success. (See R. V. Jones, chapter 44.)

Transplant

Most people feel intuitively that the driver may divert the trolley,
and some of us feel that he ought to, whereas few feel that the
surgeon may transplant organs from the healthy patient. Moreover
those of us who have these intuitions feel them very strongly,
particularly in the case of Transplant. Even if the five patients only
needed a transfusion of blood from the sixth we would not allow
the blood to be extracted without the consent of the donor: it would

constitute a criminal assault. Why, then, do we feel that it is permissible to sacrifice the single workman in Trolley when we regard it as wholly indefensible to sacrifice the patient in Transplant? How do we ground the difference?

Even if we should not 'play God', even if diverting the trolley to save the five is impermissible, we still have the problem, since the sacrifice in Transplant is very much worse.

In the trolley case we have to decide instantaneously, whereas the surgeons have a little time to think. But, in the rocket analogue, there was time to consider whether the Germans should be deceived about the rockets.

In Transplant the doctors would be breaking their Hippocratic oath, whereas there is nothing similar in the trolley and rocket cases. But why would we be so averse to modifying the oath to permit sacrifice in Transplant?

Utilitarian Approach

The side effects of a transplant practice will undermine confidence in hospitals, causing many people to forgo treatment: and this will outweigh the benefit of transplants. But: this can't fully explain the moral revulsion to Transplant: it still would be morally wrong if the side effects didn't occur.

Kantian Approach

'Never use people solely as means but also treat them as ends in themselves.'

Transplant involves using the healthy individual solely as a means to saving the others. Trolley does not involve using the single workman to save the others: it would be better if he weren't there or could jump out of the way.

A counter-example was provided by Philippa Foot: the five can be saved only by releasing a gas, which will kill the sixth;

moving the sixth would be fatal, so he would succumb to the gas. He is neither being used as a means, nor is Double Effect infringed, since the intention is to save the five.

Rational Contractors

This does not exhaust such attempts to distinguish the two; there has, for example, been appeal to rational contractors. The claim is that we would all, if rational, agree to be the single victim in Trolley, since we are more likely to be among the five saved; but that we wouldn't agree to be a sole victim sacrificed in Transplant. But if we wouldn't hypothetically consent in Transplant, why not? That still needs explaining. And if there were a culture in which people did, would it not still be wrong? We need a different approach.

An Alternative Approach

Suppose the trolley ploughs into the five, and they are taken to hospital needing transplants if they are to be saved, with the sixth man, who is temporarily in shock, but happens by extraordinary coincidence to have just the right genotype to supply the needed organs for the five. The trolley should have been diverted, perhaps, but now it is too late morally to sacrifice anyone. Why?

In civil law the initial liability principle requires loss and misfortune to lie with the victim unless there are compelling reasons to shift it to others. Doesn't the principle hold in morality too?

In Trolley, misfortune, though imminent, has yet to strike; in Transplant they have already suffered misfortune, since vital organs have been damaged and they are close to death.

This makes it easy for us to regard the turning of the trolley as the deflection or diversion of impending misfortune from many to one and the transplanting of the healthy organs as the shifting of a misfortune from several victims to another. The world we inhabit is full of risks, and bad luck is an ineluctable ingredient of human life. Once it has befallen us we do not think it right to transfer that bad luck to others without special justification. In cases where this would involve death the justification has to be very considerable.

There will be other cases in which sacrificing one to save many does not involve shifting bad luck and are nevertheless morally wrong, for example pushing someone off a bridge to halt the trolley. There are ways of treating people which are not admissible come what may.

Further Reading

William J. Fitzpatrick, 'Thomson's turnabout on the trolley', *Analysis*, 2009, vol. 69.

Philippa Foot, *Virtues and Vices*, Oxford, Blackwell, 1978.

Philippa Foot, 'Morality, action and outcome', in Ted Honderich, ed., *Morality and Objectivity*, London, Routledge and Kegan Paul, 1985.

R.V. Jones, *Most Secret War*, London, Hamilton, 1978.

Warren S. Quinn, 'Actions, intentions, and consequences: the doctrine of doing and allowing', in A. Norcross and B. Steinbock, eds, *Killing and Letting Die*, 2nd edn, New York, Fordham University Press, 1994. (Originally published in *Philosophical Review*, 1989, vol. 98.)

Judith Jarvis Thomson, 'Killing, letting die and the trolley problem', in W. Parent, ed., *Rights, Restitution, and Risk: Essays in Moral Theory*, Cambridge, Mass., Harvard University Press, 1986.

Judith Jarvis Thomson, 'Turning the trolley', *Philosophy and Public Affairs*, 2008, vol. 36.

Bernard Williams, *Ethics and the Limits of Philosophy*, London, Fontana Press, 1985.

The Two-envelope Paradox
(The Exchange Paradox)

You are presented with two sealed envelopes, A and B, and you know that one of them contains a cheque for twice as much money as the other. You are allowed to select one of them at random. You are then offered the chance to swap and take the other instead. If your selected envelope contains x, and your swap is lucky, you get $2x$, but if you are unlucky you get $0.5x$. So your expected utility if you swap is $2x/2 + 0.5x/2$, which is $1.25x$. So it looks as if you should swap.

However, exactly the same argument would have been available if you had picked the other envelope in the first place. But there can't be an expected gain from swapping A for B as well as an expected gain from swapping B for A.

What is an *expected gain*? Consider a simple case where you have two sealed envelopes, one with a cheque for a hundred euros in it and the other with a cheque for five hundred euros, but you do not know which is which. You select one of the envelopes at random. You have a 50% chance of picking the envelope with the hundred-euro cheque in and a 50% chance of picking the other one. Your expected utility is then half of €100 plus half of €500, i.e. €300.

In the case of the paradox, however, you know only that one envelope contains twice as much as the other. Assuming you want as much money as possible, do you have an interest in swapping when you have selected an envelope from the pair in which one contains twice as much as the other? What is the expected utility of swapping? If you swap, it seems you are as likely to end up with the higher sum as the lower. If your selected envelope contains x, and your swap is lucky, you get $2x$, but if you are unlucky you get $\frac{1}{2}x$. So your expected utility if you swap is a half of $2x$ plus a half of $0.5x$, which is $1.25x$, i.e. more than the x you got before swapping. For example, suppose your selected envelope has €1,000 in it. It seems that if you swap you stand to gain another €1,000, ending up with €2,000, or to lose €500, ending up with €500.

But, if you had selected the other envelope, the same argument for swapping would be available. What has gone wrong?

What has gone wrong is that the argument is fallacious. If you had been given a sealed envelope containing a cheque and offered a chance of doubling or halving it at the toss of a fair coin, there would indeed be an argument for accepting the offer. For you would then know that, if you accepted the offer, the probability of getting the higher sum was the same as the probability of the lower. If the envelope you have been given contains a cheque for x, then accepting the offer gives you 50% chance of $2x$ and a 50% chance of $0.5x$, i.e. an expected utility of $1.25x$.

So why does the argument for swapping fail in the original two-envelope case? When you first choose one of the two envelopes, you are as likely to pick the one with the smaller sum in it as the one with the larger. But it doesn't follow that, when you have picked one of them, and are offered the chance to swap, the other is just as likely to be worth twice yours as it is to be half. Yet it is difficult to see how it can fail to follow until you consider an example. Suppose the smallest cheque an envelope can contain is for €1. Then if your sealed envelopes happen to contain cheques for €1 and €2, you are as likely to pick the €1 envelope as the €2 one. Suppose you happen to pick the €1 envelope. Then it is not equally likely that the other one has €0.5 as €2: it must have a cheque for €2 inside. And if there is a finite limit to the value of a cheque, as there must be in the real world, in which there is not an infinite amount of money, then, if one of your envelopes happens to contain the maximum possible, it is obvious that it is not equally likely that the other has twice that maximum as a half.

However, you do not know whether you have one of these special cases. Couldn't the probabilities be such that the *average* expected utility of swapping was positive? No, if there is a finite limit to the amount in an envelope, this is not possible.

To see this, consider an especially simple example in which the minimum value is 1 and the other possible values are 2, 4 and 8. Let the probability that the envelopes have 1 and 2 be $2p_0$, that they have 2 and 4 be $2p_1$, and that they have 4 and 8 be $2p_2$. Then, for example, the probability of picking an envelope with 2 will be $p_0 + p_i$ (it is either one of 1 and 2, or one of 2 and 4).

	Gain	Probability
Swap 1 for 2	1	p_0
Swap 2 for 1	−1	p_0
Swap 2 for 4	2	p_1
Swap 4 for 2	−2	p_1
Swap 4 for 8	4	p_2
Swap 8 for 4	−4	p_2

The probability in the third column is the probability of the values in the first column: for example, p_0 is the probability that you have 1 in your envelope and 2 in the envelope you swap it for.

The average expected gain is calculated by calculating the weighted average of the gains in the different cases, which we do by multiplying each gain by its probability and then adding them together. Suppose a generous friend sells you an expensive lottery ticket for £1. The ticket gives you a one in a hundred chance of winning £200, and one in a thousand chance of winning £5,000. Then your expected gain from the £1 purchase is £200/100 + £5,000/1,000 less the £1 you paid, which comes to £6.

Doing this calculation for the envelopes we get: $p_0 - p_0 + 2p_1 - 2p_1 + 4p_2 - 4p_2 = 0$. And however large the maximum sum is, the weighted sum is always going to be 0, so the average expected gain from swapping is always zero. So, if there is a finite limit to the amount an envelope can contain, the paradox disappears.

The Two-envelope Paradox

But what if we remove the maximum limit, so that your envelope can contain a cheque for any amount, however large? Then it is possible to show that, if the average expectation for an envelope is nevertheless finite, the average expected gain is still zero. However, this is not invariably the case where the average expectation for an envelope is infinite. (For a simple example of an infinite expectation see **The St Petersburg Paradox**.) There are certain cases with no finite average expectation for a selected envelope where the probability distributions are such that the average expected gain is positive if it is calculated in the way described above. These are the interesting and genuinely paradoxical cases. There are three different ways of getting the average expected gain and they give different results in these cases:

(i)   What's the average expected gain from swapping given the amount in my envelope? Positive: a net gain.
(ii) What's the average expected gain given the amount in the other envelope? Negative: a net loss.
(iii) What's the average expected gain given the total in the two envelopes? Zero.

Whatever can be said in favour or against (i) can be said for or against (ii), and since only one can be right it must be (iii). But we knew that already. The problem is to explain why. One attempt to do this will be found in the paper cited below.

The paradox was introduced by Edmund Landau in 1912.

Further Reading

*Michael Clark and Nicholas Shackel, 'The two-envelope paradox', *Mind*, 2000, vol. 109.
For a non-probabilistic version of the paradox, see R. Smullyan, *Satan, Cantor and Infinity*, Oxford, Oxford University Press, 1992, pp. 189–92.

The Unexpected Examination
(The Surprise Examination, The Hangman)

A reliable teacher announces there will be a surprise exam on one weekday of the following week. The pupils reason that it can't be on Friday, since if it hasn't come by Thursday evening they will expect it the following day, and then it won't be unexpected. If it hasn't come by Wednesday evening, they will rule out Friday for the reason just given: but then it won't be a surprise on Thursday and so that day is ruled out too. And so on backwards through the week. So the teacher's announcement cannot be fulfilled.

But surely there can be a surprise exam.

The argument that there can be no surprise exam is an example of a *backward induction argument*. Despite this argument, a surprise exam is obviously a possibility, and not simply for pupils deficient in rationality or memory. We must suppose the pupils are completely rational and not suffering from any defects of memory, and that they know they are rational and have good memories. There is no paradox otherwise. That the unintelligent and the forgetful can be surprised gives rise to no logical puzzle but is a psychological commonplace.

But does the backward induction argument really get started? They know that on Thursday evening they will think, 'So either there will be an exam which I expect or there will be no exam. But in that case I can no longer be sure there'll be an exam, since the teacher's announcement cannot be fulfilled. So it could be a surprise after all. But then I must expect it, so it won't be a surprise.' This could go on round and round indefinitely. In such an unstable position the pupil cannot be sure there will be an exam, so that if an exam does take place it will be unexpected. In consequence, the argument doesn't get started. There can be a surprise exam even on Friday.

Suppose, however, the pupils can be certain there will be an exam. It is an exam which has taken place for years and it is unthinkable it will be cancelled this year. Suppose too that they still have good reason to trust the teacher and to accept it will be a surprise, although an expected exam is not as unthinkable as no exam at all. In this case the exam cannot be a surprise on Friday, because if there has been no exam by Thursday evening they will know it must occur on the final day. So the argument does get started this time, but it doesn't get very far. On Wednesday evening they will think, 'Since Friday is ruled out, there is only one possible day for the exam, tomorrow. But then we shall expect an exam tomorrow. If the teacher's word is not going to be fulfilled and the exam will be no surprise, there are still two days on which it may be held, and we have no way of choosing between them. But then it can be a surprise tomorrow, though not on Friday. But then we should expect it tomorrow, so it won't be a surprise.' This reasoning can continue indefinitely: 'But if the teacher's word is not going to be fulfilled and the exam will be no surprise, there are still two days on which it may be held . . . '. In such an unstable position they cannot be sure the exam will occur on Thursday, so they can be surprised if it is given then. After that it is too late.

In another variation the teacher says not that there will be an exam but that there will be no evening on which they will believe that *if* there is an exam it will come the next day. Reasoning parallel to that in the last paragraph shows that this cannot be fulfilled if there is no exam before Friday, but that it can be satisfied by an exam on any of the previous days.

The puzzle has been traced back to a wartime radio broadcast in Sweden in which a surprise civil defence exercise was announced for the following week.

The paradox has been assimilated to various other paradoxes. (For full details see Sorensen, cited below.) For example, self-reference has been detected as its source, since the teacher's announcement is construed as: 'You will get an unexpected exam and won't be able to deduce its date from this announcement and background information.' The one-day version, 'You will have an exam tomorrow and will not know the date in advance', is a Moorean proposition, since though not self-contradictory – it could be true – it is self-defeating in the same way as 'It is raining but I don't believe it'. (See **Moore's Paradox**.) As Sorensen shows, however, the paradox can be disentangled from self-referential and other paradoxes.

See also **The Designated Student, The Indy Paradox** and **Moore's Paradox**.

Further Reading

R. M. Sainsbury, *Paradoxes*, 3rd edn, Cambridge, Cambridge University Press, 2009, chapter 5, sections 2 and 3.

Roy Sorensen, *Blindspots*, Oxford, Clarendon Press, 1988, chapters 7, 8 and 9, and references there. Sorensen calls it 'the prediction paradox'; this name is used above for quite a different paradox.

The Paradox of Validity
(Pseudo-Scotus)

(A)
> This argument, A, is valid
> ---
> Therefore, 1 + 1 = 3

Suppose the premiss is true: then the argument is valid. Since the conclusion of a valid argument with a true premiss must be true, the conclusion of A is true. So, necessarily, if the premiss is true, the conclusion is true, which means that the argument is valid.

Since the argument is valid and its premiss is true, its conclusion must be true too: 1 + 1 = 3.

This is a variant of a paradox found in the fourteenth century writings of Albert of Saxony and of a medieval logician called Pseudo-Scotus, so called because at first his writings were wrongly attributed to John Duns Scotus. (It was the genuine Duns Scotus whose name gave rise to our term 'dunce': during the Renaissance there was a reaction against what was regarded unfairly as the hair-splitting of such medieval logicians.)

One way of dealing with this paradox exactly parallels the third approach mentioned in the discussion of **The Liar**. Any argument that includes among its premisses or conclusion a claim about its own validity or invalidity is defective, for the sentence trying to express that claim fails to express any statement. The constituent sentences, construed as referring to the argument in which they occur, fail to express any statement, true or false.

A (one-premiss) inference is valid when there is no possible situation in which its premiss is true and its conclusion is false. So, in order to know whether A is valid or not, we need to know whether there is any possible situation in which it is true that it is valid and false that $1 + 1 = 3$. This amounts to knowing whether A is possibly valid, which amounts to knowing whether it is valid, since it cannot be a mere matter of fact that it is valid. It is an a priori matter whether it is valid or not, so it is either necessary that it is valid or impossible that it should be. This means that, if it is *possible* that it should be valid, it is valid. So we cannot know whether it is valid without first knowing whether it is valid: there is no grounding for its validity or invalidity. The purported inference is not a genuine one, and the sentence which is its conclusion fails to express anything.

The conclusion of A did not have to be a necessary falsehood in order to generate the paradox. We could take any contingent falsehood as conclusion.

Consider:

(B)   This argument, B, is valid

Therefore, Paris is not the capital of France

Suppose the premiss is true. Then the argument is valid, so that its conclusion follows from its premiss. So it follows that Paris is not the capital of France.

In the paragraph above we have deduced B's conclusion from the truth of the premiss. So B is valid. Since the conclusion of a valid inference with a true premiss must be true, Paris is not the capital of France.

Pseudo-Scotus gives the paradoxical example: *God exists. Therefore this argument is invalid*, taking its premiss to be without question a necessary truth.

See also **Curry's Paradox, The Liar.**

Further Reading

W. and M. Kneale, *The Development of Logic*, Oxford, Clarendon Press, 1962, pp. 287–88.

Stephen Read, 'Self-reference and validity', *Synthese*, 1979, vol. 42.

The Paradox of Voting

It is very rare for a single vote to make any difference at all. The chance of an election being drawn or won by one vote is negligibly small, in which case the effort of voting seems a wasted one. And yet, socially and politically aware citizens are expected to vote, and assumed not to be wasting their time in doing so.

Votes in elections are rarely so close that a single vote is critical. If there is reason to think that the vote will be close, or that apathy is leading to very poor turnouts and you should set a good example, then there is obviously good reason to vote. Moreover if there is some major issue at stake which will make a huge difference to people – nuclear policy, or massive redistribution of wealth, for example – even a very small chance of causing such a huge difference will be worth taking: a one in a million chance of saving millions should be embraced. But the differences between contestants are often not so dramatic, and may be more a matter of rhetoric than substance.

Suppose a candidate you vote for wins by a majority of thousands. Your own vote may seem insignificant, but are you not as responsible for the victory as everyone else who voted for that candidate? Nevertheless, each of these voters bears only a tiny responsibility for the victory, and that may not seem enough to make it worthwhile to take the effort to go to the polling booth.

But what if everyone failed to vote? We can argue that if it is permissible for me to refrain from voting without good reason, then it is permissible for everyone else. But it can't be permissible for everyone to refrain if democracy is to be possible. Perhaps we should allow that you may refrain if you know that there will be

261

a large-enough turnout to maintain the democratic system. Then the principle on which you act would be, 'You ought to vote unless you know that enough people will vote anyway . . . '.

In voting you are expressing your political allegiance, and this may be thought worthwhile irrespective of the electoral consequences of voting. The moral significance of such expression is evident – in a negative way – in a case where someone votes for a neo-Nazi party. But voting on its own will not be a sincere expression of your political stance unless you have political allegiances, in which case you are likely to express them in other ways too. However, given strong allegiances it would normally be anomalous not to exercise your vote. Whether it has the same significance when you vote for a party that differs only in degree on major issues from its rivals is another matter.

What if you have no interest in politics? You are consumed, for example, by your work as a composer or an artist, and the work you produce is unrelated to politics. Unless widespread apathy threatens or a major issue is at stake, it may be acceptable for you not to take the trouble to vote. It is, after all, normally better that those who are interested and knowledgeable – provided their motives are not evil – should vote rather than those who are ignorant or indifferent.

Further Reading

G. Brennan and L. Lomasky, 'Toward a democratic morality', and Alvin Goldman, 'A causal responsibility approach to voting', both reprinted in D. Estlund, *Democracy*, Oxford, Blackwell, 2002.

Jonathan Glover, 'It makes no difference whether or not I do it', 1975, reprinted in P. Singer, *Applied Ethics*, Oxford, Oxford University Press, 1986.

Wang's Paradox

0 is small

If n is small, then so is $n + 1$

So every number is small

At first sight the argument certainly seems paradoxical. Numbers like one billion are scarcely small. But any natural number has only finitely many predecessors and infinitely many successors, so there is a sense in which every number is indeed small. Nevertheless, understood in the ordinary way the conclusion is false.

This paradox is really the same as the paradox of **The Heap**. The argument above is paralleled by:

If there are no grains there is no heap.
If n grains do not make a heap then neither do $n + 1$ grains.
So no quantity of grains makes a heap.

This is simply Argument II in the entry on **The Heap**, given in reverse, except that it starts with 0 instead of 1. For discussion, see that entry.

See also **Quinn's Paradox.**

Further Reading

*Michael Dummett, 'Wang's paradox', reprinted in Rosanna Keefe and Peter Smith, eds, *Vagueness: A Reader*, Cambridge, Mass. and London, MIT Press, 1997.

The Xenophobic Paradox
(The Medical Test)

In a town where only one person in ten is black, a man claims he was mugged by a black person. In re-enactments of the scene under comparable lighting with different people playing the assailant, he identified the assailant's race correctly 80% of the time. Members of either race are equally likely to mug.

But his chance of being right about the race of the assailant who mugged him is less than one in three.

It is natural to think that, if the man has an 80% chance of having correctly identified the colour of his assailant, and claims he was mugged by a black man, he is more likely to be right than wrong. But, on the contrary, he is more likely to be wrong than right, for his chance of being right is only $^4/_{13}$. That is the probability that the assailant was black given that he was identified as black.

This is because the chance that an assailant should be black and correctly identified as such is only 80% multiplied by 10% (the proportion of blacks), or $0.8 \times 0.1 = 0.08$. The chance that the assailant is white but identified as black is $0.2 \times 0.9 = 0.18$. So blacks are identified on 26% of occasions, but only correctly on 8% of them. (We are assuming for the sake of simplicity that the chance of correctly identifying an individual's colour is the same for both whites and blacks, 80%.)

In a representative sample of 100 there will be 10 blacks. Two of these will be misidentified as white; 18 of the remaining 90 will be misidentified as black. Since 8 of the 10 blacks will be identified correctly but 18 whites will be wrongly identified as black, the probability that the assailant is black, given that he is identified as black, is only $^8/_{26}$, or little over 30%.

264

The point is that the higher the proportion of whites, the greater the chance of misidentifying whites as black, as is evident from the table below, which shows how the chance of being right that the assailant is black rises with the proportion of blacks. Indeed if the community is 100% black the identification of the assailant as black is bound to be right: he couldn't be anything else.

The same applies with the proportion of whites, of course. If they are in the minority they will be misidentified more often.

Accuracy of identification of blacks rises with increasing proportion of blacks

Proportion of blacks (%)	0.00	0.10	1.00	10.00	20.00	25.00	50.00	75.00	100
Blacks correctly identified (%)	0.00	0.40	3.88	30.77	50.00	57.14	80.00	92.31	100

80% of identifications correct. Formula to compute proportion of blacks identified correctly:

$0.8 \times proportion\ of\ blacks/(0.8 \times proportion\ of\ blacks + 0.2\ (1 - proportion\ of\ blacks))$.

Comparing this table with the similar table for **Simpson's Paradox** brings out an affinity with it, albeit that the structure of the latter is more complex, involving as it does misleading aggregation.

It is easy to see how xenophobia may be induced by misinterpreting figures for minority ethnic groups. The misinterpretation is very common and not at all obvious at first sight.

The paradox comes in many guises. Here is an exactly parallel medical example, where for simplicity we keep the same figures.

Let the incidence of a certain disease be 10%. Medical tests for it are 80% accurate: so that 20% of the positive outcomes are false positives and 20% of the negative outcomes false negatives. (Assume for the sake of simplicity that the incidence is the same for those tested. In any case, all that matters for the present discussion is the incidence among those tested. So if you want to make the example more realistic you can allow that the incidence in the general population is lower.)

Your doctor tells you that you have tested positive and that the test is 80% accurate. What is the chance you have the disease? Extraordinarily, it's not at all as high as you might think: it's not 80%, it's little more than 30%! In a representative sample of 100, where the incidence is 10%, there will be 10 with the disease. If all are tested, 8 of the diseased 10 will get a correct positive result; 18 of the remaining 90 will get a false positive result. That makes 26 positives, of which 8 are correct. So the probability that you have the disease, given that your test is positive, is $^8/_{26}$ = 30.77%.

As we can see from the table above, if the incidence of the disease is only 1% (a more usual sort of figure) a positive test means you have less than 1 chance in 25 (less than 4%) of having the disease. And if the incidence is 1 in 1,000 (perhaps even more usual) the chance is 1 in 250. If not only you but also your doctor think the chance is 80%, you may agree to possibly hazardous treatment which would not be warranted by a 0.4% chance. And yet in a survey the majority of medical doctors and nurses gave the wrong answer for a similar example.

See also **Simpson's Paradox.**

Further Reading

Scientific American, March 1990, p. 119.

Yablo's Paradox

Imagine an infinitely long sequence of sentences:

(YI) All the following sentences are untrue.

(Y2) All the following sentences are untrue.

   ⋮

(Y*n*) All the following sentences are untrue.

   ⋮

You will find that you cannot consistently assign the values 'true' or 'false' to the members of this sequence.

One of the examples of **The Liar** paradox given above, Buridan's ninth sophism, is cyclical, and so indirectly self-referential:

Socrates: (*S*) 'What Plato is saying is false.'

Plato: (*P*) 'What Socrates is saying is true.'

We can generalize this to produce longer indirectly self-referential loops:

(S1) The following sentence is untrue.

(S2) The following sentence is untrue.

(S3) The following sentence is untrue.

   ⋮

(S*n*) The first sentence is true.

These will have to be alternately true and false: TFTF . . . or FTFT . . . Since S1 has to be true if S*n* is true, and false if S*n* is false, we get a paradox in the cases where *n* is even, since in those cases S1 and S*n* will have different truth values. (If *n* is odd, the list is paradoxical in the way the truth-teller is, since there is no way of choosing between the two alternative assignments. But set those cases aside here.)

Yablo's Paradox

Stephen Yablo's paradox involves an *infinite* sequence of sentences:

(Y1) All of the following sentences are untrue   ← Suppose true. Then all the sentences from Y2 onwards are untrue, which is impossible.

← Suppose false. Then at least one of the following sentences is true. Every sentence following that one will have to be untrue, which is impossible.

(Y2) All of the following sentences are untrue.

(Y3) All of the following sentences are untrue.

$$\vdots$$
$$\vdots$$

Yablo claims that, unlike other versions of the liar, this paradox does not involve self-reference, since each sentence is about those following it and no sentence is about itself. But each sentence seems to be implicitly self-referential, since 'all of the following sentences' has in each case to be understood as 'all the sentences following this one'. (Yablo actually refers to the following sentences by 'for all $k > n$', where n is the current subscript to Y, but self-reference is still arguably implicit there.)

But, whether self-referential or not, we clearly have a paradox here. See the entry on **The Liar** for possible resolutions: on the third approach canvassed there, none of the sentences in the infinite sequence can be allowed to express a statement.

Further Reading

J. C. Beall, 'Is Yablo's paradox non-circular?', *Analysis*, 2001, vol. 61.

Stephen Yablo, 'Paradox without self-reference', *Analysis*, 1993, vol. 53.

Zeno's Paradoxes

See Achilles and the Tortoise, The Arrow, The Paradox of Plurality, The Racecourse.

See also The Trojan Fly, The Paradox of the Gods, The Numbered Balls.

Index

Index

Index

Index

Index

Index

www.routledge.com/philosophy

Available from *The Basics* Series

Logic: The Basics

Jc Beall, University of Connecticut, USA

'Beall has achieved a rare combination of lucidity and sophistication. This book is a marvelous introduction to philosophical logic that engages the issues without getting bogged down in formalities. Anyone looking to explore what lies beyond a first course in logic must read this book.' – Colin Caret, *University of St Andrews, UK*

Logic: The Basics is a hands-on introduction to the philosophically alive field of logical inquiry. Covering both classical and non-classical theories, it presents some of the core notions of logic such as validity, basic connectives, identity, 'free logic' and more. This book:

- Introduces some basic ideas of logic from a semantic and philosophical perspective
- Uses logical consequence as the focal concept throughout
- Considers some of the controversies and rival logics that make for such a lively field.

This accessible guide includes chapter summaries and suggestions for further reading as well as exercises and sample answers throughout. It is an ideal introduction for those new to the study of logic as well as those seeking to gain the competence and skills needed to move to more advanced work in logic.

Published 19 March 2010 by Routledge – 184pp
Pb: 978-0-415-77499-4

Available from all good bookshops

Thinking from A to Z

Third Edition

Nigel Warburton, *The Open University, UK*

'Warburton is always a very clear writer and has the knack
of finding the right register to talk to the non-professional
without over-simplifying or patronising.' – *Philosopher's
Magazine*

What is 'humpty-dumptying'? Do 'arguments from analogy' ever stand
up? How do I know when someone is using 'weasel words'? What's
the difference between a 'red herring' and a 'straw man'?

This superb book, now in its third edition, will help anyone who
wants to argue well and think critically. Using witty and topical
examples, this fully-updated edition includes many new entries and
updates the whole text. New entries include:

- Principle of Charity
- Lawyer's Answer
- Least Worst Option
- Poisoning the Well
- Sentimentality
- Sunk Cost Fallacy
- Weasel Words
- 'You would say that wouldn't you'.

Thinking from A to Z may not help you win every argument, but it will
definitely give you the power to tell a good one from a bad one.

Published 27 June 2007 by Routledge – 176pp
Pb: 978-0-415-43371-6